D0945472

The Body Remembers

The Psychophysiology
of Trauma and
Trauma Treatment

A NORTON PROFESSIONAL BOOK

The Body Remembers

The Psychophysiology of Trauma and Trauma Treatment

BABETTE ROTHSCHILD

W. W. Norton & Company
New York • London

page 26: *I Remember It Well* from GIGI. Words by Alan Jay Lerner. Music by Frederick Loewe. Copyright © 1957, 1958 by Chappell & Co. Copyright Renewed. International Copyright Secured. All Rights Reserved.

Piet Hein Grooks © Rhyme and Reason (p. 37), Timing Toast (p. 77), A Toast (p. 100) are reproduced with kind permission from Piet Hein a/s, DK-5500 Middelfart, Denmark.

The author welcomes correspondence from readers. She may be reached at:
Babette Rothschild
P.O. Box 241778
Los Angeles, California 90024
Telephone: 310-281-9646
Fax: 310-281-9729
E-mail: babette@trauma.cc
Web site: www.trauma.cc

Copyright © 2000 by Babette Rothschild
All rights reserved
Printed in the United States of America
First Edition

For information about permission to reproduce selections from this book, write to Permissions, W. W. Norton & Company, Inc., 500 Fifth Avenue, New York, NY 10110

The text of this book is composed in Fairfield with the display set in Fairfield
Composition by Dori Miller Design
Manufacturing by Haddon Craftsmen

Library of Congress Cataloging-in-Publication Data

Rothschild, Babette
    The body remembers: the psychophysiology of trauma and trauma treatment / Babette Rothschild.
        p.   cm. — (Norton professional book)
    Includes bibliographical references and index.
    ISBN 0-393-70327-4
        1. Post-traumatic stress disorder—Psychological aspects. 2. Mind and body therapies. 3.
    Post-traumatic stress disorder—Physiological aspects. I. Title. II. Series.
    RC489.M53 R68 2000
    616.85'21—dc21   00-062520

W. W. Norton & Company, Inc., 500 Fifth Avenue, New York, N.Y. 10110
www.wwnorton.com

W. W. Norton & Company, Ltd., 10 Coptic Street, London WC1A 1PU

2 3 4 5 6 7 8 9 0

For Margie

Contents

Acknowledgments

It is not possible to tackle the arduous project of writing a professional book without being taught, helped, influenced, inspired, and advised by others. Those who have crossed my path in the 28 years since my entry into the psychotherapy field are too numerous to mention individually, though all have contributed in some way. Collectively, I would like to thank each of the teachers, therapists, supervisors, and researchers who have helped me to shape my opinions into a serviceable form. Those who have most influenced my thinking with regard to trauma theory and treatment are acknowledged by reference within the pages of this text. Nonetheless, I would like to particularly recognize Lisbeth Marcher and her colleagues at Denmark's Bodynamic Institute, Peter Levine, and Bessel van der Kolk. They have had a profound influence on the evolution of the ideas expressed in these pages. I would also like to express my grateful thanks to the many trainees, supervisees, students and clients who have all, in ways both small and large, contributed to the content of this book. Like many, I have learned—and continue to learn—the most from those I have had the privilege to teach and treat.

I would like to express gratitude specifically to Karen Berman, Danny Brom, Alison Freeman, Michael Gavin, David Grill, John May, Yvonne Parkins, Gina Ross, and Sima Juliar Stanley for their brutally critical comments on this manuscript. In addition, I want to thank life sciences writer, Karin Rhines, for being such a great "coach" throughout this project. Her knowledge of the business of writing, as well as her uncanny ability to know just when to cheer and when to chide, has been invaluable.

I consider myself to be a very fortunate author to have Norton Professional Books as my publisher. Having previously read many grateful acknowledgments to my editor, Susan Munro, I now know what everybody was talking about. In addition to being a skilled, patient, and good-humored editor, her knowledge of my subject matter as well as her command of the professional literature has been an invaluable bonus. In fact, I have been heartened by my contacts with all of the staff I have encountered at W.W. Norton—on both sides of the Atlantic. They have each and all contributed to making the writing of this book a pleasure.

Introduction

The Body Remembers is intended as a complement to existing books on the theory and treatment of trauma and posttraumatic stress disorder and to the existing methods of trauma therapy. It is hoped that it will add the dimension of understanding and treating the traumatized *body* to the already well-established knowledge of and interventions for treating the traumatized *mind*. Psychotherapists working with traumatized clients will in all likelihood find that the theory, principles, and techniques presented within these pages are consistent with and applicable to the therapy model(s) in which they are already trained. In addition, they should find that the information presented here can be used and adapted without conflict with, or abandonment of, their preferred principles or techniques.

ON BUILDING BRIDGES

The Body Remembers is meant to be a bridge-building book. It is my hope to traverse at least two of the deep chasms within the field of traumatology. The first bridge spans the gap between the theory developed by scientists, particularly in the area of neurobiology, and the clinical practice of therapists working directly with traumatized individuals and groups. The second bridge aims to connect the traditional verbal psychotherapies and those of body-oriented psychotherapy (body-psychotherapy).

The gaps between mind and body, traditional psychotherapy and body-psychotherapy, and between theory and practice have long been of concern to me. Increasingly I have found that posttraumatic stress disorder (PTSD) is forcing a bridging of these gaps. Even the most conservative of therapists and researchers acknowledges that PTSD is not just a psychological condition, but also a disorder with important somatic components. Moreover, all professionals who deal with PTSD find that they must stretch their theories and practice. Both psychotherapists and body-psychotherapists are pressed to pay greater attention to neurobiologic theory and to account for and treat somatic symptoms, the body-psychotherapist must also find ways to work without touch and to increase verbal integration, and the researcher is being challenged to make more pertinent connections between theory and practice. It is my hope that *The Body Remembers* will facilitate meaningful links in bridging these gaps.

Science vs. Practice

"A Widening Gulf Splits Lab and Couch" read the headline of the *New York Times*' Women's Health section on June 21, 1998 (Tavris, 1998). Most psychotherapists knew it, but many of my colleagues were surprised to see such criticism in print. Not a few were offended. The author of that article, Carol Tavris, claimed that "'psychological science' is an oxymoron." She criticized practitioners for paying too little attention to science, often being more focused on technique than theory. Most of the professionals I have spoken with agree with Carol Tavris that scientific theory and practice are usually too divergent to be relevant when they are sitting with a client. I, however, believe that this gap between scientist and practitioner is one of semantics rather than principles. The language of the scientific literature is often difficult to read and comprehend, though much that is being offered is extremely relevant, if difficult to translate into the language of practice.

I have endeavored in *The Body Remembers* to present theory in an easily accessible form that is relevant to direct practice. By so doing, I hope to narrow the chasm between the neuroscientist and behavioral researcher studying the phenomenon of trauma and the psychotherapist working directly with the traumatized client.

Theory is the most valuable tool of the trauma therapist, because understanding the mechanisms of trauma as proposed by psychological, neurobiological, and psychobiological theory greatly aids treatment. The greater a therapist's theory base, the less dependence there will be on techniques learned by rote. Thorough understanding of the neurological and physiological underpinnings of the trauma response and the development of PTSD will enable on-the-spot creation and/or adaptation of interventions that are appropriate and helpful to a particular client, with his* particular trauma. A theoretical foundation also aids therapists in applying techniques learned from various disciplines, choosing and enhancing those that have the best chance of success in each unique situation. The therapist well versed in theory is able to adapt the therapy to the client, rather than assuming the client will fit into the therapy.

Psychotherapy vs. Body-psychotherapy

It is my additional hope that this book will build a bridge between the practitioners of traditional verbal psychotherapies and the practitioners of body-oriented psychotherapies. I believe that these two professional groups have much to offer each other in the treatment of trauma and PTSD.

The first encouragement I came upon for traversing this chasm was Bessel van der Kolk's seminal article, "The Body Keeps the Score," in the *Harvard Review of Psychiatry* (van der Kolk, 1994). It was in this article that I first found the body-mind connection legitimized in mainstream psychiatry. In addition, Antonio Damasio's *Descartes' Error* (1994) has been a great inspiration. This groundbreaking book presents a neurological, theoretical basis for the mind-body connection. Both of these works have laid the foundation for my understanding of the psychophysical, neurobiological relationship between the mind and the body. Further, the recent work of Perry, Pollard, Blakley, Baker, and Vigilante (1995), Schore (1994, 1996), Siegel (1996, 1999), van der Kolk (1998), and others on infant attachment, brain development, and memory systems has tremendous implications for our understanding of how trauma could so adversely disrupt the nervous system that an individual would develop PTSD.

Bridging the gap between the verbal psychotherapies and the body-psychotherapies means taking the best resources from both, rather than choosing one over the other. Integrated trauma therapy must consider, consist of, and utilize tools for identifying, understanding, and treating trauma's effects on both mind and body. Language is necessary for both. The somatic

---

* I have attempted to alternate the use of the pronouns he, she, him, her, his, and hers throughout the text. I hope I have been equitable.

disturbances of trauma require language to make sense of them, comprehend their meaning, extract their message, and resolve their impact. When healing trauma, it is crucial to give attention to both body and mind; you can't have one without the other.

WORKING WITH THE BODY DOES NOT REQUIRE TOUCH

Touching the body and working with the body are not, and need not be, synonymous when it comes to psychotherapy or, for that matter, body-psychotherapy. There are many ways to work with the body, integrating important aspects of muscular, behavioral, and sensory input, without intruding on bodily integrity.

There are many reasons not to use touch as a part of psychotherapeutic or body-psychotherapeutic treatment. Aside from the obvious concerns about the possible effect on the transference, there is the question of respect for client boundaries, particularly with clients who have been physically or sexually abused. Equally worthy of consideration is the personal preference of the client and the personal preference of the therapist. In addition, many malpractice insurance policies will not cover treatment methods that use touch and the licensing boards of most U.S. states forbid it. Do not get me wrong. I am not an extremist. In some cases I think judicious touch can be useful when client and therapist agree, but in this book I focus on body techniques that do not involve touch, since those are, in my opinion, the most appropriate for use with traumatized clients.

THE FALSE MEMORY CONTROVERSY

This is *not* a book about false memories, and I make no claims about, nor have any ambition to resolve, the current controversy. However, as this book involves the subjects of memory and trauma, I cannot avoid giving voice to my opinion on this explosive and difficult issue.

My opinion is inclusive: I believe early memories of trauma can sometimes be recovered with relative accuracy, and I am also equally convinced that sometimes false memories can be inadvertently created or encouraged—by the therapist as well as the client. I have been witness to examples of both with clients and trainees, friends and family, and even myself.

Somatic memory, a primary concern of this book, is, in my opinion, neither more nor less reliable than any other form of memory—as will be discussed later in this book. Somatic memory can be continuous, and it can also be "forgotten," just like cognitive memory. It can also be distorted, as it is the mind that interprets and misinterprets the body's message. The mind, of course, is subject to a wealth of influences that can alter the accuracy of a memory over time.

Though I offer no solutions to the controversy, I hope that *The Body Remembers* will provide assistance in two areas: helping the therapist to be more alert to and cautious of the risk of false memories, and offering tools for identifying, understanding, and integrating what the body actually does remember.

The International Society for Traumatic Stress Studies has struggled with this controversy for several years. In 1998 it published a monograph on the issue, *Childhood Trauma Remembered* (ISTSS, 1998). That concise publication gives a balanced view of this controversy, and I highly recommend it.

ORGANIZATION OF THIS BOOK

This book is organized into two major sections. Part I, *Theory*, presents and discusses a theory for understanding how the human mind and body process, record, and remember traumatic events and what can impede as well as facilitate these faculties. The current and most convincing evidence from neuroscience and psychobiology is included, as well as theories that have survived the test of time. In Part II, *Practice*, strategies for helping the traumatized body, as well as the traumatized mind, are presented. Non-touch tools for helping survivors of trauma to make sense of, as well as ease, their somatic symptoms are offered. The proffered tools are consistent with and applicable to any model of therapy geared to working with traumatized individuals.

A DISCLAIMER

The scientific study of the mechanisms of trauma, PTSD, and memory is accelerating at such a fast pace that it is impossible to keep up. There are sometimes strong disagreements between scientific groups. What causes and what heals PTSD and how memory systems function are subject to broad debate. The research-supported theories of one group are disputed by another and vice versa. For better or worse, at least on the topics of trauma and memory, science seems to be a matter of opinion.

Therefore, what you have here are my considered opinions based on sometimes divergent theories. No clear-cut truths are to be found among these pages because they do not, yet, exist. I hope, however, there will be a great deal that is thought-provoking and useful. I trust each reader will formulate his or her own considered opinions.

Neurologist Antonio Damasio eloquently states similar sentiments in his introduction to *Descartes' Error*. I believe his words are worthy of repetition: "I am skeptical of science's presumption of objectivity and definitiveness. I have a difficult time seeing scientific results, especially in neurobiology, as anything but provisional approximations, to be enjoyed for a while and discarded as soon as better accounts become available" (1994, p. xviii).

This is a minimalist book—short-winded—as I want anyone who is interested to have the time to tackle it. Among these pages you will find comprehensible theories and applicable techniques that will be useful with many, though not all, of your clients—all told, what I believe to be the best of the (as Damasio would say) current approximations.

The Body Remembers

The Psychophysiology
of Trauma and
Trauma Treatment

PART ONE

Theory

CHAPTER ONE

Overview of Posttraumatic Stress Disorder (PTSD)

The Impact of Trauma on Body and Mind

If it is true that at the core of our traumatized and neglected patients'
disorganization is the problem that they cannot analyze what is going
on when they re-experience the physical sensations of past trauma,
but that these sensations just produce intense emotions without
being able to modulate them, then our therapy needs to consist of
helping people to stay in their bodies and to understand these bodily
sensations. And that is certainly not something that any of the tradi-
tional psychotherapies, which we have all been taught, help people
to do very well.

—Bessel van der Kolk (1998)

That the body remembers traumatic experiences is aptly illustrated by the
following case of "Charlie and the Dog."* This case is presented in several parts, beginning with this first part that introduces Charlie's traumatic
event and his resulting somatic and psychological symptoms. In subsequent
chapters, the interventions that helped Charlie to resolve the impact of the
traumatic incident will be detailed. In addition, illustrative references to Charlie will be woven throughout the text, providing a common thread connecting
the theory and practice elements of this book.

---

* For the sake of protecting privacy and confidentiality all identifying information has been
altered in every case example and session vignette throughout this book. For the same reason,
many of the cases presented are actually composites of several cases. In each instance the
basic principles and thrust of the therapy being presented have been maintained.

CHARLIE AND THE DOG, PART I

A few years ago, out for a leisurely Sunday afternoon bicycle ride on a country lane, Charlie's pedaling reverie was suddenly broken as a large dog began to chase him, barking furiously. Charlie's heart rate soared, his mouth went dry, and his legs suddenly had more power and strength than he had ever known. He pedaled faster and faster, but the dog matched and then exceeded his pace. Eventually the dog caught up and bit Charlie on his right thigh. As Charlie and his bike tumbled, the dog continued his barking attack. Charlie lost consciousness. Luckily, he had landed in a public area where several people rushed to his aid, chasing off the dog and calling an ambulance. Charlie's leg healed quickly, unlike his mind and nervous system. He continued to be plagued each time he saw a dog. Just the sight of one, even when locked in a house, behind a door, a window, and a fence, would cause Charlie to break into a cold sweat, go dry in his mouth, and feel faint. Since that incident he had kept his distance from all dogs, even pets of friends, avoiding contact whenever possible. He would habitually cross the street to evade a dog on his side of the street, whether on the sidewalk or behind a fence. He would never encourage contact, never talk to or stroke a dog. As time passed, Charlie's life became more and more restricted as he attempted to avoid any and all contact with dogs.

Then, once, during a training session at a retreat center, Charlie was unexpectedly confronted with his worst fear. He sat comfortably on a cushion listening to a lecture, focused on the lecturer (who stood to his left) and not on his surroundings. Unbeknownst to Charlie, the center's canine mascot, Ruff, had joined the group. Ruff quietly approached uninvited from Charlie's right (outside of his field of vision) laid down, and gently placed her head on Charlie's right leg, hoping for a pat. Charlie, feeling the weight on his right leg, looked down and caught a glimpse of Ruff out of the corner of his right eye. He then immediately, and literally, froze in panic. Charlie's mouth went dry, his heart rate soared, and his limbs stiffened to the extent that he was totally unable to move. He was barely able to speak.

Charlie's reaction to Ruff was not just in his mind. Rationally, Charlie remembered the dog attack and knew that he was scared of dogs. He also knew that Ruff was not attacking him. But all of his rational thoughts appeared to have no effect on his nervous system. Charlie's body reacted as if he was being, or about to be, attacked again. He became paralyzed. What is it that occurred in

Charlie's brain and body that caused such an extreme reaction in the absence of an actual threat? Why was Charlie unable to move or push the dog away? Why did he continue to go dry in the mouth and break into a cold sweat at the mere sight of a dog at a protected distance? What could be done to help Charlie cease these extreme reactions in the presence of dogs? Answering these questions provides the underpinning of *The Body Remembers*.

A Basic Premise

Trauma is a psychophysical experience, even when the traumatic event causes no direct bodily harm. That traumatic events exact a toll on the body as well as the mind is a well-documented and agreed-upon conclusion of the psychiatric community, as attested in the *Diagnostic and Statistical Manual of Mental Disorders, 4th Edition,* of the American Psychiatric Association (*DSM-IV*). A major category in the symptom list of posttraumatic stress disorder (PTSD) is "persistent symptoms of increased arousal" in the autonomic nervous system (ANS) (APA, 1994). Yet, despite a plethora of study and writing on the neurobiology and psychobiology of stress, trauma, and PTSD, the psychotherapist has until now had few tools for healing the traumatized body as well as the traumatized mind. Attention directed at the body has tended to focus on the distressing symptoms of PTSD, the resulting problems of adaptation, and possible pharmacological intervention. Using the body itself as a possible resource in the treatment of trauma has rarely been explored. Somatic memory has been named as a phenomenon (van der Kolk, 1994), but few scientifically supported theories and strategies for identifying it, containing it, and making use of it in the therapeutic process have emerged.

Understanding how the brain and body process, remember, and perpetuate traumatic events holds many keys to the treatment of the traumatized body and mind. In some instances, direct somatic interventions, when used as adjuncts to existing trauma therapies, can be powerful in combating the effects of trauma. In addition, various somatic techniques can be used to make any therapy process easier to pace and less volatile. Attention to the somatic side of trauma need not require the practitioner to change his direction or focus. The tools offered here can be used or adapted within existing models of trauma therapy, expanding and enhancing what is already being done.

THE SYMPTOMATOLOGY OF PTSD

PTSD disrupts the functioning of those afflicted by it, interfering with their abilities to meet daily needs and perform the most basic tasks. In PTSD a traumatic event is not remembered and relegated to one's past in the same way as other life events. Trauma continues to intrude with visual, auditory, and/or other somatic reality on the lives of its victims. Again and again they relive the life-threatening experiences they have suffered, reacting in mind and body as though such events were still occurring. PTSD is a complex psychobiological condition. It can emerge in the wake of life-threatening experiences when psychological and somatic stress responses persist long after the traumatic event has passed.

There is a mistaken assumption that anyone experiencing a traumatic event will develop PTSD. This is far from true. Results of studies vary but in general confirm that only a fraction of those facing such incidents—around 20%—will develop PTSD (Breslau, Davis, Andreski, & Peterson, 1991; Elliott, 1997; Kulka et al., 1990). What distinguishes those who do not is still a controversial topic, but there are many clues. Nonclinical factors that mediate traumatic stress appear to include: preparation for expected stress (when possible), successful fight or flight responses, developmental history, belief system, prior experience, internal resources, and support (from family, community, and social networks).

In the history of psychology, PTSD is a relatively new diagnostic category. It first appeared in 1980 in the internationally accepted authority on psychology and psychodiagnosis, *Diagnostic and Statistical Manual of Mental Disorders*, 3rd Edition (*DSM-III*; APA, 1980). *DSM-III*'s definition of what could cause PTSD was limited. It was seen as developing from an experience that anyone would find traumatic. There were at least two problems with this definition: It left no room for individual perception or experience of an event, and it mistakenly assumed that everyone would develop PTSD from such an event. The currently accepted definition, as revised in *DSM-IV* (APA, 1994), is much broader. This definition takes into account that PTSD can develop in an individual in response to three types of events: (1) incidents that are, or are perceived as, threatening to one's own life or bodily integrity; (2) being a witness to acts of violence to others; or (3) hearing of violence to or the unexpected or violent death of close associates. Events that could qualify as traumatic for both adults and children, according to *DSM-IV*, include combat, sexual and physical assault, being held hostage or imprisoned, terrorism, torture, natural and man-made disasters, accidents, and receiving a diagnosis of a life-threatening illness. In addition, *DSM-IV* notes that PTSD can develop in children who have experienced sexual molestation, even if this is not life-threatening. It adds, "The disorder may be especially severe or long lasting when the stressor is of human design (e.g., torture, rape)" (APA, 1994, p. 424).

Symptoms associated with PTSD include (1) reexperiencing the event in varying sensory forms (flashbacks), (2) avoiding reminders of the trauma, and (3) chronic hyperarousal in the autonomic nervous system (ANS). *DSM-IV* recognizes that such symptoms are normal in the immediate aftermath of a traumatic event. PTSD is first diagnosed when these symptoms last more than one month and are combined with loss of function in areas such as one's job or social relationships.

Somatic disturbance is at the core of PTSD. People who suffer from it are plagued with many of the same frightening body symptoms that are characteristic of ANS hyperarousal experienced during a traumatic incident (*as was Charlie*): accelerated heart rate, cold sweating, rapid breathing, heart palpitations, hypervigilance, and hyperstartle response (jumpiness). When chronic, these symptoms can lead to sleep disturbances, loss of appetite, sexual dysfunction, and difficulties in concentrating, which are further hallmarks of PTSD. *DSM-IV* acknowledges that symptoms of PTSD can be incited by external *as well as* internal reminders of a traumatic event, cautioning us that somatic symptoms, alone, can trigger a PTSD reaction. PTSD can be a very vicious circle.

DISTINGUISHING STRESS, TRAUMATIC STRESS, PTS, AND PTSD

Hans Selye defined stress as, "the nonspecific response of the body to any demand" (1984, p. 74). Generally regarded as a response to negative experiences, stress can also result from desired, positive experiences, such as marriage, moving, a job change, and leaving home for college.

The most extreme form of stress is, of course, stress that results from a traumatic incident—*traumatic stress. Posttraumatic stress* (PTS) is traumatic stress that persists following (post) a traumatic incident (Rothschild, 1995a). It is only when posttraumatic stress accumulates to the degree that it produces the symptoms outlined in *DSM-IV* that the term posttraumatic stress *disorder* (PTSD) can be applied. PTSD implies a high level of daily dysfunction. Though there are no statistics, one can guess that there are a significant number of trauma survivors with PTS, those who fall between the cracks—not recovered from their traumas, but without the debilitation of PTSD. These individuals can also benefit from trauma therapy. (*Charlie's level of disturbance is typical of PTS. It caused him restriction in one area of his life— avoidance of dogs—but he functioned normally in the rest of his life.*)

SURVIVAL AND THE NERVOUS SYSTEM

Arousal, and therefore traumatic hyperarousal, is mediated by the limbic system, which is located in the center of the brain between the brain stem and the cerebral cortex. This part of the brain regulates survival behaviors and emotional expression. It is primarily concerned with tasks of survival, such as eating, sexual reproduction, and the instinctive defenses of fight and flight. It also influences memory processing.

The limbic system has an intimate relationship with the autonomic nervous system (ANS). It evaluates a situation, signaling the ANS either to have the body rest or to prepare it for effort. The ANS plays a role in regulating smooth muscles and other viscera: heart and circulatory system, kidneys, lungs, intestines, bladder, bowel, pupils. Its two branches, the sympathetic branch (SNS) and the parasympathetic branch (PNS), usually function in balance with each other: When one is activated, the other is suppressed. The SNS is primarily aroused in states of effort and stress, both positive and negative. The PNS is primarily aroused in states of rest and relaxation.

The limbic system responds to the extreme of traumatic threat, by releasing hormones that tell the body to prepare for defensive action (see Figure 1.1, p. 10). Following the perception of threat, the amygdala signals an alarm to the hypothalamus (both structures in the limbic system) that turns on two systems: (1) activation of the SNS, and (2) the release of corticotropin-releasing hormone (CRH). Those actions continue, each with a separate, but related, task. First, the activation of the SNS will, in turn, activate the adrenal glands to release epinephrine and norepinephrine to mobilize the body for fight or flight. This is accomplished by increasing respiration and heart rate to provide more oxygen, sending blood away from the skin and into the muscles for quick movement. (*In Charlie's case, the increased respiration and blood flow to his legs made it possible for him to pedal faster and farther than usual.*) At the same time, in the other system, the CRH is activating the pituitary gland to release adrenocortio-tropic hormone (ACTH), which will also activate the adrenal glands, this time to release a hydro-cortizone, cortisol. Once the traumatic incident is over and/or the fight or flight has been successful, the cortisol will halt the alarm reaction and the production of epinephrine/norepinephrine, helping to restore the body to homeostasis.

This system is called the HPA axis. The reason it is important to trauma work is that in PTSD something goes wrong with it. Rachel Yehuda (Yehuda et al., 1990) pioneered the discovery that in those with PTSD the adrenal glands do not release enough cortisol to halt the alarm reaction (see Figure 1.2). Several studies have shown that individuals with PTSD have lower cortisol levels than controls, even those with other psychological problems like depression (Bauer, Priebe, & Graf, 1994; Yehuda et al., 1990, 1995; Yehuda, Teicher, Levengood, Trestman, & Siever, 1996). One conclusion that can be drawn from this evidence is that on a chemical level the continued alarm reaction typical of PTSD is due to a deficiency of cortisol production. However, whether it is a purely biological process or is influenced by perception in the limbic system is not known. While the low cortisol levels are documented in PTSD, their cause is still a question.

One area of interest with regard to the HPA axis and cortisol is the freezing response to traumatic threat. When death may be imminent, escape is impossible, or the traumatic threat is prolonged, the limbic system can simultaneously activate the PNS, causing a state of freezing called *tonic immobility*—like a mouse going dead when caught by a cat, or stiff, like a deer caught in headlights (Gallup & Maser, 1977). The chemical picture that causes the freeze must be linked to the HPA axis, but this has not been studied as yet.

These nervous system responses—fight, flight, and freeze (or tonic immobility)—are automatic survival actions. They are similar to reflexes in that they are instantaneous, but the mechanisms underlying these responses are much more complex than simple reflexes. If the perception in the limbic system is that there is adequate strength, time, and space for flight, then the body breaks into a run. If the limbic perception is that there is not time to flee but there is adequate strength to defend, then the body will fight. If the limbic system perceives that there is neither time nor strength for fight or flight and death

Figure 1.1. Hypothalamic-pituitary-adrenal (HPA) axis.

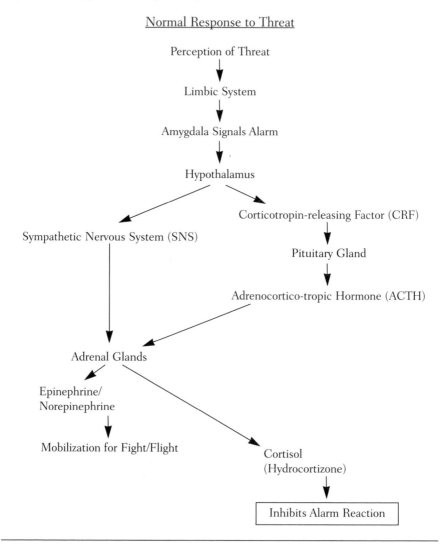

could be imminent, then the body will freeze. In this state the victim of trauma enters an altered reality. Time slows down and there is no fear or pain. In this state, if harm or death do occur, the pain is not felt as intensely. People who have fallen from great heights, or been mauled by animals and survived, report just such a reaction. The freeze response might also increase chances of survival. If the cause is an attack by man or beast, the attacker may lose interest once the prey has gone dead, as a cat will lose interest in a lifeless mouse.

Figure 1.2. Hypothalamic-pituitary-adrenal (HPA) axis.

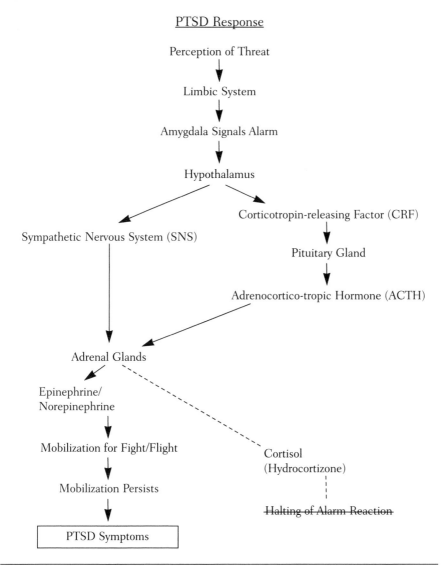

PTSD Response

Perception of Threat

Limbic System

Amygdala Signals Alarm

Hypothalamus

Corticotropin-releasing Factor (CRF)

Sympathetic Nervous System (SNS)

Pituitary Gland

Adrenocortico-tropic Hormone (ACTH)

Adrenal Glands

Epinephrine/
Norepinephrine

Mobilization for Fight/Flight

Cortisol
(Hydrocortizone)

Mobilization Persists

Halting of Alarm Reaction

PTSD Symptoms

(*Charlie lost consciousness during the dog attack, and when later confronted by contact with a dog he became paralyzed. Both are forms of freezing responses.*)

It is important to understand that these limbic system/ANS responses are instantaneous, instinctive responses to perceived threat. They are not chosen by thoughtful consideration. Many who have suffered trauma feel much guilt and shame for freezing or "going dead" and not doing more to protect themselves or

back or running away. In those instances, understanding that
ic often facilitates the difficult process of self-forgiveness.

DEFENSIVE RESPONSE TO REMEMBERED THREAT

When the limbic system activates the ANS to meet the threat of a traumatic event, it is a normal, healthy, adaptive survival response. When the ANS *continues to be chronically aroused* even though the threat has passed and has been survived, that is PTSD. The traumatic event seems to continue to float free in time, rather than occupying its locus in one's past, often coming unbidden into the present perception as if it were, indeed, occurring now. (*Charlie was never again attacked by a dog. However, each time he encountered one he continued to respond in his mind and body as if he were being, or about to be, attacked again.*)

Within the limbic system are two related areas that are central to memory storage: the hippocampus and the amygdala. The last few years have produced a growing body of research that indicates these two parts of the brain are centrally involved in recording, filing, and remembering traumatic events (Nadel & Jacobs, 1996; van der Kolk, 1994, among others). The amygdala is known to aid in the processing of highly charged emotional memories, such as terror and horror, becoming highly active both during and while remembering a traumatic incident. The hippocampus, on the other hand, gives time and space context to an event, putting our memories into their proper perspective and place in our life's time line. Hippocampal processing gives events a beginning, a middle, and an end. This is very important with regard to PTSD, as one of its features is a sense that the trauma has not yet ended. It has been shown that the activity of the hippocampus often becomes suppressed during traumatic threat; its usual assistance in processing and storing an event is not available (Nadel & Jacobs, 1996; van der Kolk, 1994, among others). When this occurs, the traumatic event is prevented from occupying its proper position in the individual's history and continues to invade the present. The perception of the event as being over and the victim as having survived is missing. This is the likely mechanism at the core of the quintessential PTSD symptom of "flashback"—episodes of reliving the trauma in mind and or body.

DISSOCIATION, FREEZING, AND PTSD

Surprisingly, dissociation, a splitting in awareness, is not mentioned by either the *DSM-III* or *DSM-IV* as a symptom of PTSD, though it is acknowledged as a symptom of acute stress disorder (APA, 1994). There is a growing debate as to whether PTSD is actually a dissociative disorder, rather than an anxiety disorder as it is currently classified (Brett, 1996). At the International Society for Traumatic Stress Studies a panel debated this issue (Wahlberg, van der Kolk, Brett, & Marmar, 1996). No one really knows what dissociation is or how it occurs, though there is much speculation. It appears to be a set of related forms of split awareness. The wide range of splitting covers events as simple as forgetting why you were going into the kitchen and as extreme as dissociative identity disorder (previously called multiple personality disorder). The kind of dissociation described by those with PTSD during their traumatic event(s)— altered sense of time, reduced sensations of pain, absence of terror or horror— resembles the characteristics of those who report having responded by freezing to a traumatic threat. There will need to be more research before it can be known if the freezing response is a form of dissociation.

Understanding this mechanism is important because it appears that the most severe consequences of PTSD result from dissociation. While dissociation appears to be an instinctive response to save the self from suffering—and it does this very well—it exacts a high price in return. There are several areas of research into the phenomenon of dissociation. Many indicate the likelihood that dissociation during a traumatic event (peritraumatic dissociation) predicts the eventual development of PTSD (Bremner et al.,1992; Classen, Koopman, & Spiegel, 1993; Marmar et al., 1996).

CONSEQUENCES OF TRAUMA AND PTSD

The consequences of trauma and PTSD vary greatly depending on the age of the victim, the nature of the trauma, the response to the trauma, and the support to the victim in the aftermath. In general, those afflicted with PTSD suffer reduced quality of life due to intrusive symptoms, which restrict their ability to function. They may alternate periods of overactivity with periods of exhaustion as their bodies suffer the effects of traumatic hyperarousal of the ANS. Reminders of the trauma they suffered may appear suddenly, causing instant panic. They become fearful, not only of the trauma itself, but also of their own reactions to the trauma. Body signals that once provided essential information become dangerous. For example, heart rate acceleration that might indicate overexertion or excitement can become a danger signal in itself because it is a reminder of the accelerated heart rate of the trauma response, and is therefore associated with trauma. The ability to orient to safety and danger becomes decreased when many things, or sometimes everything, in the environment are perceived as dangerous. When daily reminders of trauma become extreme, freezing or dissociation can be activated as if the trauma were occurring in the present. It can become a vicious cycle. Eventually, a victim of PTSD can become extremely restricted, fearing to be with others or to go out of her home. (*As mentioned before, Charlie had PTS not PTSD; the degree of his restriction never reached this extreme. However, he was becoming increasingly restricted with each fearful canine encounter, and the potential for developing PTSD lingered.*)

How is it possible for the mind to become so overwhelmed that it is no longer able to process a traumatic event to completion and file it away in the past? The next chapters move toward possible answers to that question.

CHAPTER TWO

Development, Memory, and the Brain

In many instances, people who experience traumatic events are able to process and resolve those episodes free of long-term effects. They are able to recall and narrate the events that befell them, make sense of what happened, have emotions appropriate to their memories, and feel confident that the incident lies in their past.

In people still plagued by their traumas, those with PTS and PTSD, memory of traumatic events is different. It usually falls into one of two divergent categories. Some traumatized people will remember the traumatizing events in precise detail, able to describe what happened as if they were watching a video replay. In these cases PTS or PTSD persists because these individuals are not able to make sense of the events, or some aspect of them. They may still be disturbed by intense emotions and/or bodily sensations seemingly unconnected to the traumas they suffered. (*Charlie's memory of the dog attack is an example. He remembered the details up to the point where he lost consciousness, but continued to feel in danger each time he was in the vicinity of a dog, no matter how benign that dog was.*) Or they might feel numb in body and/or emotions and complain of a sense of deadness in their lives. Others remember little if any of the actual traumatic events but are plagued by physical sensations and emotional reactions that make no sense in the current context. Whether the trauma is remembered or not, for those with PTS and PTSD the realization that it lies in the past and that the danger is over is attained only with difficulty.

A look into how the brain develops may reveal clues to help us understand these types of memory distortion.

THE DEVELOPING BRAIN

The newborn's brain is by no means a fait accompli, not even close. At birth the brain is among the most immature of the body's organs. In fact it is much like a new computer, equipped with a basic operating system that incorporates all that will be needed for future development and programing, memory file storage and expansion, but as yet unable to do much beyond the basic system requirements.

The human brain is, for the most part, malleable—programmable and reprogrammable—in its organization. It is highly responsive to external influences. In fact, the higher and more complex the brain structure, the greater its malleability (Perry, Pollard, Blakley, Baker, & Vigilante, 1995). The cerebral cortex is the most complex, as well as the most flexible and easily influenced, structure. The brain stem is the least complex and least malleable structure in the brain. The brain's susceptibility to influence and change is necessary to growth and development. Without the ability of our brains to adapt and change, it would be impossible to learn anything. Growth, development, and change are necessary to health and to survival. Though it remains flexible throughout the lifespan, the brain's capacity for alteration does decrease with age. And, of course, the first days, months, and years of life are crucial for establishing the foundations of later capacities and talents, as well as deficits.

How a brain first organizes is dependent on the infant's interactions with its environment. How a brain continues to grow, develop, and reorganize is dependent on the subsequent experiences encountered throughout a child's life. As no two life experiences are the same, even for identical twins, it is the brain's malleability that makes each of us unique. Recognizing that the brain's organization is flexible and subject to influence is crucial to understanding both how dysfunctional emotional patterns, such as PTSD, can develop and how they can be changed.

From the Beginning

The infant brain has the instincts and reflexes that are needed for existence (heartbeat, respiration reflex), the ability to take in and make use of nourishment (search, suck, and swallow reflexes; digestion and elimination) and to benefit from contact (sensory pathways, grasp reflexes), etc. This basic brain system, though, is not enough to ensure the infant's survival. The baby needs a more mature human (the primary caretaker—usually, but not always, its mother) to care for and protect it. Moreover, many believe it is the interaction between baby and caretaker that determines normal brain and nervous system development.

None of this is new. Babies depend on their caregivers for every aspect of their survival. Caregivers who are able to provide for infants' emotional as well as physical needs nurture them into toddlers, children, teens, and adults with a wide scope of resources. Increasingly they are able to take over caring for their own needs in adaptive and beneficial ways. Well-cared-for babies become adults with resilience who are able to swing with the punches dished out by life. Their brains are able to process and integrate both positive and negative experiences, adding adaptive learning to their repertoire of behaviors and attitudes.

On the other hand, babies raised by caregivers unable to meet significant portions of their needs are at risk of growing into adults who lack resilience and have trouble adapting to life's ebbs and flows. Their brains may be less able to process life's experiences. They appear to have more difficulty making sense of life's events, particularly those that are stressful, and to be more vulnerable to psychological disturbances and disorders, including drug addiction, depression, and PTSD (Schore, 1994).

There is a growing body of research that describes how healthy bonding and attachment are crucial to healthy development from the first days of life (Schore, 1994; Siegel, 1999; van der Kolk, 1998). The attachment relationship stimulates brain development which, in turn, expands and enables an individual's ability to cope emotionally throughout life. Science is finally catching up with parents and psychotherapists, who have always known that this was true but didn't know why or how. It is now believed that the nurturing interaction between caregiver and infant goes a long way in promoting healthy emotional development, because that relationship, in itself, stimulates normal maturation of the brain and nervous system.

A Few Basics

What follows is a very brief overview of how the brain develops. Later chapters will expand on these basics. The material included here will be limited to what is necessary for the purpose of understanding how brain development eventually affects the processing of traumatic incidents.

The brain is the control center of the nervous system. It regulates body temperature, tells us when to seek nourishment, and directs all the functions involved in eating, digestion, and elimination. It tells our heart to beat and causes us to inhale and exhale. Without the brain, procreation would be impossible and the human species would die out. In addition, the brain, like a computer, processes information. It receives information through all of the body's sensory pathways: sight (which includes written words), hearing (which includes spoken words), taste, touch, smell, proprioception (which informs on the body's spatial and internal states), and the vestibular sense (which indicates which way is up).

Nervous System Communication

The term *synapse* (see Figure 2.1) refers to a junction of two nerve cells (neurons). It is at this site that the signal or information from one nerve transfers to the next, as if a spark jumps the gap. The communication from the one cell to the next can be accomplished with either an electrical impulse or via a chemical neurotransmitter that passes from one cell to the other. Epinephrine and norepinephrine are examples of neurotransmitters. These hormones are secreted in response to traumatic stress (see "Survival and the Nervous System" in Chapter 1), epinephrine by the sympathetic nerves in the adrenal glands, norepinephrine by the sympathetic nerves in the rest of the body (Sapolsky, 1994). When enough norepinephrine secretes from the sympathetic nerve endings along the path from synapse to synapse, the body is readied to fight or flee.

Strings of synapses link neurons in configurations that produce the complex activities that are carried out by the brain and the body. Each string of synapses produces a single result: the contraction of a muscle, the recall of an image, the blink of an eye, the stomach sensation of butterflies, one heartbeat, the gasp of surprise. Combinations of synapse strings produce more complicated results: walking, talking, solving a math problem, understanding a written paragraph, remembering the details of a movie, realizing one is cold and turning up the heat. All of the information coming into the body and brain through the senses is realized and registered through discrete sets of synapses, and each reflex, behavior, emotion, or thought is produced through discrete sets of synapses. All experiences are encoded, recorded, and recalled through

Figure 2.1. Synapse.

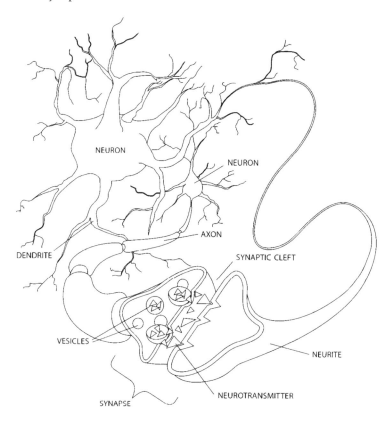

Reprinted with permission from the Press Office of the Charles A. Dana Foundation.

synapses. The brain regulates all body processes and behaviors through synapses that connect efferent nerves (brain → body). Likewise, the body reports back to the brain on its internal state and position in space through synapses connecting afferent nerves (body → brain). It is also through sets of synapses that individual thoughts become linked as concepts or tied to specific events. Cognitive memory involves the linking of the nerves via synapses within the brain. Somatic memory requires that sensory nerves be linked via synapses to the brain and then recorded within the brain.

There is nothing fixed about the sequence of synapses, however. They are subject to influence and can be changed. New learning is achieved through the creation of new synapse strings, or adaptation of existing ones. Forgetting (e.g., how to do something) is the result of disuse of synapse strings—as the saying goes, "use it or lose it." It is also, for better or worse, through the alteration of synapses that memory can become distorted.

Divisions of the Brain

It is easy to conceptualize what the brain looks like (see Figure 2.2). Make your right hand into a fist, holding it upright. Your right wrist represents the brain stem, your fist the midbrain and limbic system. Now take your left hand and cover your right fist. That is the cerebral cortex, the outer layer of the brain.

The *brain stem*, sometimes referred to as the *reptilian brain*, regulates basic bodily functions such as heart rate and respiration. This region of the brain must be mature at birth for an infant to survive.

The *limbic system* is the seat of survival instincts and reflexes. It includes the hypothalamus, which is responsible for maintaining body temperature, essential nutrition and hydration, rest and balance. The limbic system also regulates the *autonomic nervous system*, mediating smooth muscle and visceral responses to stress and relaxation, including sexual arousal and orgasm, and the traumatic stress reactions of fight, flight, and freeze. Two other limbic system regions, the *hippocampus* and the *amygdala,* are especially pertinent to understanding traumatic memory. Both the hippocampus and the amygdala consist of two lobes, one on each side of the brain. Both structures are integral to processing information transmitted from the body on the way to the cerebral cortex.

The amygdala processes and then facilitates the storage of emotions and reactions to emotionally charged events. The hippocampus processes the data necessary to make sense of those experiences within the time line of personal history (i.e., "When during my life did this happen?") and the sequence of the experience itself (i.e., "What happened first? What happened next?" etc.). Nadel and Zola-Morgan (1984) have found that the amygdala is mature at birth, and that the hippocampus matures later, between the second and third year of life. Understanding the difference in the maturational schedules, as well as the functions of these two structures, provides one explanation for the phenomenon of *infantile amnesia*—the fact that we usually don't consciously remember our infancy. Infantile experiences are processed through the amygdala on the way to storage in the cortex. The amygdala facilitates storage of the emotional and sensory content of these experiences. Hippocampal function is not yet available, so the resulting memory of an infantile experience includes

Figure 2.2. Divisions of the brain.

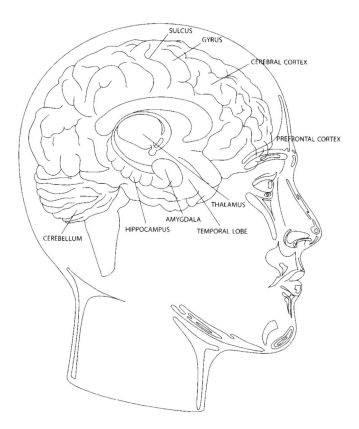

Reprinted with permission from the Press Office of the Charles A. Dana Foundation.

emotion and physical sensations without context or sequence. This is the probable explanation for why, in later life, infantile experiences cannot be accessed as what we usually call "memories" (Nadel & Zola-Morgan, 1984).

Mature and adequate function of both amygdala and hippocampus is necessary for sufficient processing of life's events, especially the stressful ones, though during a traumatic event this may not always be possible. As the stress level increases, hormones may be released that suppress hippocampal activity, while the amygdala remains unaffected. It is possible that prolonged cortisol secretion, as may be found with trauma, affects the hippocampus in this way (Gunnar & Barr, 1998). This might account for some of the memory distortion associated with PTSD. Some individuals with PTSD recall their traumatic experiences as highly disturbing emotional and sensory states, lacking the time and space context that is facilitated by hippocampal function. Hippocampal size has been the subject of recent PTSD research. Several studies conclude that survivors of PTSD have smaller hippocampi than the general population (among others: Bremner et al., 1997; Rauch, Shin, Wahlen, & Pitman, 1998; Schuff et al., 1997). These fascinating findings have not determined, however, whether the hippocampi of those with PTSD have shrunk due to suppression of hippocampal activity by stress hormones or whether these individuals had smaller hippocampi to begin with. At any rate, it appears that smaller hippocampus size might interfere with the brain's processing of stressful life events.

The *thalamus* is also part of the midbrain; its two parts flank the limbic system. It is the relay center for sensory information coming from all points in the body on the way to the cortex.

Overlaying the more primitive structures of the brain is the *cerebral cortex,* which is responsible for all higher mental functions, including speech, thought, and semantic and procedural memory. Currently there is great interest in the various information-processing functions of the right and left cortices and their relationship to the limbic system. The right cortex appears to play a greater role in the storage of sensory input. It appears that the amygdala is the limbic structure through which sensory information travels on its way to the right cortex. The left cortex, on the other hand, seems to have a more intimate relationship with the hippocampus. Moreover, it appears to depend on language for processing information. Bessel van der Kolk (van der Kolk, McFarlane, & Weisaeth, 1996) has found that activity in Broca's area, which is a left cortical structure responsible for speech production, is also suppressed (as is the hippocampus) during a traumatic incident. He describes what he calls the "speechless terror" of trauma. We have all experienced being at a loss for words or forgetting what we were about to say. Under stress this difficulty increases, sometimes to extreme degrees. (*In Charlie's case, he could still speak in his panicked state, but the speech apparatus was so constricted that he could barely squeak his words out.*)

Mutual Connection and the Developing Brain

Allan Schore (1994) and Bruce Perry (Perry et al., 1995) have both proposed neurological models for understanding the importance of infant attachment in the mediation of stressful experiences throughout life. According to both models, the primary caretaker, in addition to providing for an infant's basic needs, plays a crucial role in helping the infant to regulate sometimes very high levels of stimulation. A healthy attachment between infant and caretaker enables the infant to eventually develop the capacity to self-regulate both positive and negative stimuli. Perry and his colleagues (1995) further propose that positive early experiences are crucial to optimal organization and development of specific brain regions.

The newborn infant is a bundle of raw sensory receptors. For nine months the fetus is swathed and insulated in its mother's amniotic fluid. Though there are sensory stimuli in utero, they are dampened. The newborn is ill-prepared for the sudden inundation of stimuli at birth. Suddenly it is literally propelled into an environment full of new and intense sensations of touch, sound, taste, sight, smell, cold, heat, and pain. The infant screams in response to this first flood of stimuli. But when placed on its mother's belly, hearing her familiar (if previously muffled) voice, and feeling her loving touch, perhaps even smelling her familiar scent, the newborn is quickly soothed. This is the infant's first experience of stimulus regulation mediated by its primary caretaker. The baby's mother has (usually), in an instant, been able to intercede and quell the overwhelming inundation of multiple new stimuli, calming the child. And so it goes, ideally, throughout infancy. The baby is upset, and the caretaker's presence soothes.

At first the caretaker helps the child regulate its responses to stimuli, including being uncomfortable from hunger, thirst, wetness, cold, pain, etc. Gradually, the caretaker also assists the child in regulating her emotional responses: frustration, anger, loneliness, fear, and excitement. In the beginning, much of the regulation process takes place through touch and sound. However, as Schore (1996) describes, quite soon after birth the caretaker and infant develop an interactional pattern that is central to the process of affect regulation. They learn to stimulate each other through face-to-face contact, which enables the infant gradually to acclimate to greater and greater degrees of stimulation and arousal.

These interactions between the caretaker and infant—bonding and attachment, upset and regulation, stimulus and attunement—are, Schore believes, all right-brain mediated. During infancy the right cortex is developing more quickly than the left—and, as previously stated, the left-brain associated hippocampus is still immature (Schore, 1996).

Toward the end of the first year, the relationship between primary caretaker and baby changes drastically. The baby makes its first movements into toddlerhood—creeping, crawling, and eventually standing and walking—and develops greater independence and possibilities for interaction with the environment. Simultaneously, the caretaker's role changes from being nearly 100% nurturing, approving, and soothing into a regulator of socialization who sets limits, says "no," and sometimes disapproves and/or causes pain. How caretaker and child resolve this change in roles depends on at least three factors: the solidity of the attachment bond, the capacity of the caretaker for continued love despite becoming angry at the child's misbehaviors, and the ability of the caretaker to set and maintain balanced and consistent limits. It is also around this time that the left cortex begins an accelerated growth period that continues as language, a left cortical function, develops. Meanwhile, in the limbic system, the hippocampus matures, enhancing the child's capacity to make sense of his environment. With a sound beginning, founded in a secure attachment, and later rational, consistent limit-setting, the child will begin to use his growing language to describe events and make sense of his emotional and sensory experiences.

The Developing Brain and Trauma

Why are some individuals more easily disturbed by traumatic events than others? Schore (1996), van der Kolk (1987, 1998), Siegel (1999), De Bellis and colleagues (1999), Perry and colleagues (1995), and others assert that predisposition to psychological disturbance, including PTSD, can be found in stressful events during early development: neglect, physical and sexual abuse, failure of the attachment bond, and individual traumatic incidents (hospitalization, death of a parent, car accident, etc.). There is speculation that individuals who suffered early trauma and/or did not have the benefit of a healthy attachment may have limited capacity for regulating stress and making sense of traumatic experiences later in their lives. In some, it is possible that reduced hippocampal activity, either because it was never fully developed (attachment deficit) or because it became suppressed (traumatic events), limits their ability to mediate stress (Gunnar & Barr, 1998). Under those circumstances, later traumatic experiences might be remembered by some only as highly charged emotions and body sensations. In others, it may be that survival mechanisms such as dissociation or freezing have become so habituated that more adaptive strategies either never develop or are eliminated from the survival repertoire.

The Mature Brain and Trauma

Even when infancy and childhood have gone well, even ideally, an adolescent or adult may confront a traumatic event so overwhelming that PTS or PTSD results. Some of the most convincing evidence for this comes from studies of Holocaust survivors who were settled in post World War II Norway. Like the other Scandinavian countries, Norway played an important role in the recovery and resettlement of thousands of survivors of the German concentration camps. In addition to meeting their basic needs for medical attention, nutrition, and clean and safe living quarters, the Norwegians provided psychiatric support. Until WWII, Norwegian psychiatry, similar to its European and American counterparts, regarded mental illness as developing from childhood deficits. As symptoms of mental illness were prevalent among the concentration camp survivors, the Norwegian psychiatrists expected to hear childhood histories riddled with dysfunction. They were astonished to find that most of the survivors reported happy childhoods in cohesive, supportive families. What could account for such a disparity? The psychiatrists were eventually compelled to conclude that the evidence "convincingly demonstrated that chronic mental illnesses could develop in persons who had a harmonious childhood but who had been subjected to extreme physical and psychological stress" (Malt & Weisaeth, 1989, p. 7). Thus, the aftermath of the Holocaust marked a drastic change in how psychiatry viewed the effects of extreme stress on adults. (*Charlie also illustrates this theory, as his trauma occurred when he was an adult. He developed PTS following the dog attack—and was well on his way to PTSD as his life became more restricted. Charlie's reaction was not due to earlier trauma or to developmental deficits.*)

Hopeful Implications for Psychotherapy

Infancy is not the only chance an individual has for a healthy attachment. A traumatized infant is not necessarily condemned to dysfunction. For example, many children who were deprived of a good infantile relationship do, to a large extent, make up for that lack later in life—with a best friend, special teacher, or comforting neighbor. And many adolescents and adults find a healing bond within a mature love relationship. For many, such relationships go a long way to compensate for what they missed or suffered as infants. Still others find the needed bond in the psychotherapeutic relationship. (The role of dynamic psychotherapy and body-psychotherapy in the compensation of early deficits and healing of early and massive trauma will be addressed in Chapter 5.)

Brain maturation provides the foundation for acquiring necessary skills and resources, including recognizing and applying the lessons of life's events. How the brain processes and remembers traumatic incidents will determine who does and who does not develop PTSD. The quality of the infant-caregiver attachment is an important, though not the only, variable involved in predicting healthy brain maturation. In the following section, categories of memory and their relationship to the brain and to the development of PTSD will be discussed.

WHAT IS MEMORY?

We met at nine. We met at eight.
I was on time. No, you were late.
. . . Ah, yes, I remember it well . . .
—GIGI

Research into memory—the function of memory and memory systems—is a rapidly expanding field of study. It has been accelerating since the 1960s and reached a furious, sustained pace in the early 1990s. Among the reasons for this increased interest is the controversy over traumatic memory recall.

The Basics of Memory

In general, memory has to do with the recording, storage, and recall of information perceived from the internal and external environments. All of the senses are integral to how the world is perceived. The brain processes perceptions and stores them as thoughts, emotions, images, sensations, and behavioral impulses. When these stored items are recalled, that is memory.

For a piece of information to become a memory it must traverse at least three major steps: *encoding* is the process of recording or etching information onto the brain; memory *storage* is how and for how long that information is kept; and memory *retrieval* accesses the stored information, bringing it back into conscious awareness. Actually, the process of brain memory is quite similar to computer memory. Writing words on a screen encodes information onto the computer. But that is only a temporary measure unless it is saved in a file, which is akin to memory storage. Once saved in a file, that information lies dormant until retrieved by reopening the file (recall). As with brain memory, a saved computer file can sometimes be difficult to relocate.

Some types of information are more likely to be stored than others. The greater the significance, and the higher the emotional charge—both positive and negative—the more likely a piece of information (or an event made up of multiple pieces of information) will be stored (Schacter, 1996).

The Long and the Short of It

As recently as 40 years ago, memory was thought to be only one thing: either we remembered or we didn't. What we now call *long-term memory* was the only category recognized. When memory failed it was called forgetting or, in the extreme, amnesia. It was thought that our experiences were etched on the brain's cortex as on a videotape. Memory was the video playback. This theory was supported by the brain-stimulation studies conducted by Wilder Penfield. These well-known experiments are fascinating, but possibly misleading. While operating on epileptic patients, Penfield randomly stimulated areas of the brain's temporal lobe and recorded the "memories" reported by his patients (Penfield & Perot, 1963). Some reported astoundingly detailed sensory-laden images. Penfield has, however, been criticized for exaggerating his discovery. It appears that fewer than 10% of his patients actually reported "memories" during direct brain stimulation and none of those were validated: There was no way to distinguish genuine memory from induced hallucination (Squire, 1987).

Around 1960, scientists began to speculate about two different systems of memory: long-term memory and a new category called *short-term memory*. At that time there was no theory for *where* in the brain those types of memory resided or what brain systems were responsible for them. However, it was clear that short-term memory depended on a different brain system than long-term memory. This was the birth of the idea of multiple memory systems in the brain, which is now the norm (Nadel, 1994, Schacter, 1996).

It is short-term memory that is used to remember a phone number from the time it is seen or heard until it is dialed, test answers after "cramming" the night before an exam, and a waiter's face. Such items usually slip quickly from one's grasp, just as words written onto the computer screen are quickly lost if they are not saved in a file. And that appears to be a good thing, preventing the brain from becoming cluttered with an abundance of unnecessary information—10 years of nightly dinners, every advertising jingle, etc. It is short-term memory that often frustratingly begins to weaken with age, "What was that I was just about to do?" "It was on the tip of my tongue . . ."

Long-term memory is just what the name implies. It involves items of information that are permanently stored—whether or not they are ever recalled into consciousness.

However, there is much more to memory than the length of time an item of information is stored. Understanding *which* items are stored, *where* they are stored, and *how* the brain accomplishes storage are all necessary to further comprehend memory.

The Implicit and the Explicit

In the late 1980s and early 1990s the idea of multiple memory systems became widely accepted. An important discovery during this time was two new types of memory: *explicit* and *implicit*. These two disparate memory systems distinguish what types of information are stored and how they are retrieved. Table 2.1 contrasts the explicit and implicit memory systems.

Explicit Memory

Explicit memory is what we usually mean when we use the term "memory." Sometimes called *declarative memory*, it is comprised of facts, concepts, and ideas. When a person thinks consciously about something and describes it with words—either aloud or in her head—she is using explicit memory. Explicit memory depends on oral or written language, that is, words; language

Table 2.1. Categories of memory.

	EXPLICIT = DECLARATIVE	IMPLICIT NONDECLAR
Process	conscious	unconscious
Information types	cognitive	emotional
	facts	conditioning
	mind	body
	verbal/semantic	sensory
	description of operations	automatic skills
	description of procedures	automatic procedures
Mediating limbic structure	hippocampus	amygdala
Maturity	around 3 years	from birth
Activity during traumatic event and/or flashback	suppressed	activated
Language	constructs narrative	speechless

This table is similar to one in Hovdestad and Kristiansen, 1996, p. 133.

is necessary to both the storage and the retrieval of explicit memories. An opinion, an idea, a story, facts of a case, narration of Sunday dinner at Grandma's—all are examples of items of information that would be stored in explicit memory. Explicit memory is not just facts, however; it also involves remembering operations that require thought and step-by-step narration, as in solving a mathematical equation or baking a cake. It is explicit memory that enables the telling of the story of one's life, narrating events, putting experiences into words, constructing a chronology, extracting a meaning.

Explicit memory of a traumatic event (or any event, for that matter) involves being able to recall and recount the event in a cohesive narrative. Another aspect of explicit storage involves historical placement of an event in the proper slot of one's lifetime. Currently, there is speculation that some incidences of PTSD may be caused, in part, when memory of a traumatic event is somehow excluded from explicit storage.

Implicit Memory

Where explicit memory depends on language, implicit memory bypasses it. Explicit memory involves facts, descriptions, and operations that are based on thought; implicit memory involves procedures and internal states that are automatic. It operates unconsciously, unless made conscious though a bridging to explicit memory that narrates or makes sense of the remembered operation, emotion, sensation, etc.

Implicit memory, first called *procedural* or *nondeclarative* memory, has to do with the storage and recall of learned procedures and behaviors. Without implicit procedural memory, accomplishing some tasks would be at best laborious, at worst impossible. Bicycle riding provides a good example. Implicit memory makes it possible to ride a bike without thinking about it. While there may be an explicit memory of the time when riding a bike was learned—often with Mom or Dad holding the back of the seat and running alongside—one does not usually utilize explicit narrative memory while riding a bicycle. Relying only on explicit memory to ride a bike, it would be necessary to construct a narrative, following each step as you might a recipe:

> *I stand to the right of the bike, facing it. I take hold of the handlebars with my hands. Then, keeping my right foot on the ground, I lift my left leg over the top, landing awkwardly with my left buttocks on the seat; the bike tipped to the right. I keep holding onto the handlebars with both hands, bend my right knee and push off the ground with my right foot. Simultaneously, I shift the weight on my buttocks to the left so it becomes centered on the seat. Quickly, I apply pressure to the left pedal, pushing it forward and then down. As I do that, the right pedal, with my right foot on it, moves backwards and up. When it reaches the top, I tilt the right pedal with my right foot, toes pointed upward, and push it forward and down. I continue the forward and down pressure on one pedal at a time. The bike moves forward. I keep straight on the seat, controlling my balance by keeping my head upright and letting my hips move from side to side . . .*

No one approaches riding a bicycle with such explicit narration. They would never get anywhere. Clearly, explicitly remembering such a procedure is a laborious process. Implicit memory certainly has many advantages.

However, when it comes to memory of traumatic events, implicit memories not linked to explicit memories can be troublesome. It appears that traumatic events are more easily recorded in implicit memory because the amygdala does not succumb to the stress hormones that suppress the activity of the hippocampus. No matter how high the arousal, it appears that the amygdala continues to function. In some cases, upsetting emotions, disturbing body sensations, and confusing behavioral impulses can all exist in implicit memory without access to information about the context in which they arose or what they are about.

Conditioned Memory

A class of implicit memory includes behavior learned through *classical conditioning* (CC) or *operant conditioning* (OC). These theories may be familiar, as they are usually taught in basic psychology courses. Either or both of them can be involved in the learned trauma responses of those with PTS and PTSD.

Classical Conditioning

Classical conditioning, discovered by Ivan Pavlov, involves pairing a known stimulus with a new, conditioned stimulus (CS) to elicit a new behavior called a conditioned response (CR). In Pavlov's famous experiment, he taught a hungry dog to respond physiologically to a bell as though it were food. He repeatedly rang a bell (CS) just before presenting food (S) to the dog. Of course, it salivated—a normal response (R)—at the sight and smell of the food. That sequence was repeated many times. Eventually the bell became associated with the food. Pavlov then removed the stimulus of the food and only rang the bell. Again the dog would salivate (CR). It was no longer necessary to present the dog with food to elicit the now conditioned response (Pavlov, 1927/1960). What had once been a normal response to the stimulus of food became a conditioned response to a bell:

> bell → association to food → salivation, *becomes* bell → salivation

Classical conditioning is especially germane to the discussion of PTSD. It is likely that this process is the mechanism underlying the phenomenon of *traumatic triggers.* To put it simply, during a traumatic event, many cues can become associated with the trauma. Those same cues can later elicit a similar response (CR). For example, if a woman is raped (S) by a man in a red (CS) shirt and is very afraid (R), she may later become fearful (CR) when she sees the color red (CS). If enough information about the rape was recorded explicitly in her brain, she may be able to make the connection and reduce her reaction, "Oh yes, the color red frightens me because it reminds me of the time I was raped." However, even if she doesn't remember one or more items of information, she could still have a reaction. That is one consequence of classically conditioned implicit memory: automatic reactions in the absence of cognitive, factual thought. In the case of trauma, the reaction is very distressing. Triggers (in this case, the color red) often cause intense reaction. A person is unaware of the cause unless the association is made, either spontaneously or with the help of psychotherapy.

An additional problem with the phenomenon of triggers is that they can be very difficult to track down. Classical conditioning can create chains of conditioned stimuli such that an individual trigger (CS) may be several generations away from the original stimulus-response scenario. The dog who learned to salivate at the sound of the bell could be taught to salivate to a flashing light just by pairing the bell to the light (second CS). The same could happen following the above example of rape. At a later time, the same woman walks down a street past a fabric store. In the window is an array of red (first CS) material. A few steps past the store her heart starts beating rapidly (CR) and she feels dizzy. She doesn't know what is happening to her and her anxiety escalates into a panic attack. If she has no conscious clue to what caused the panic, she might reach for an explanation that makes sense and conclude (consciously or unconsciously) that something on that street must be dangerous or unsafe. She may later avoid walking on that street (second CS). If this pattern continues without intervention, she might eventually have a panic attack just from going out on any street (third CS) and become agoraphobic, unable to go out at all without knowing why. Now this, of course, is not the only explanation for agoraphobia, but it is a very plausible scenario of how it could develop. Classically conditioned associated generations of traumatic triggers can cause increasingly greater degrees of restriction, avoidance, and, eventually, debilitation. (*Charlie generalized his fear of the type of dog that attacked him [CS] to all dogs [second CS]—no matter what they looked like [large/small] or how they acted [aggressive/docile]. His life became restricted as the sight of any dog, even at a distance or on its owner's leash, caused his heart to race and his skin to break out in a cold sweat.)*

Memory in the Absence of Memory. Classical conditioning helps to clarify how it is possible to react to a reminder of a traumatic event without recalling that event. An interesting case from the early days of psychology provides a simple, yet fascinating illustration.

A female patient of the early 20th century French physician Edouard Claparede was unable to create new memories due to brain damage. Each time the doctor met this patient, it was as if it was for the first time. She never remembered him, even if the last time she had seen him was just a few minutes before. Curious, Dr. Claparede devised an experiment. One time he entered the examining room holding out his hand in customary greeting; however, that time, he hid a tack in his palm. As usual, she took his hand, but she withdrew it immediately in response to the surprise of pain. When the doctor subsequently visited the patient, she refused to shake hands with him, but could not say why (Claparede, 1911/1951).

Familiarity with the theory of memory systems makes understanding this seemingly phenomenal occurrence quite simple. Claparede's patient was, indeed, able to create new memories, just not explicit ones. Through classical conditioning a previously neutral behavior (hand shaking) had become paired with a conditioned stimulus (pain), causing a conditioned response (recoiling in pain and fear). It only took one time to condition the response. The very next time the doctor appeared, the patient refused to take his hand (conditioned response). Her implicit memory system was fully intact (no pun intended). Her hand remembered being the painful prick and her arm remembered recoiling. She did not want to do that again. She did recognize and remember the doctor, though not in the normal way that we conceptualize recognition and memory.

Operant Conditioning

Operant conditioning, first known from the work of B. F. Skinner, involves shaping behavior through a cause and effect system of positive and/or negative reinforcement. Behavior modification is based on operant conditioning. In a typical Skinner-type experiment a bird is taught to depress a pedal with its beak to receive food. It is rewarded with a few grains each time it performs the desired behavior, in this case pedal pecking. Eventually the behavior becomes automatic. What starts out as a random occurrence—the first time the bird accidentally depressing the pedal—quickly becomes associated and learned through rewards of food. The bird is then able to deliberately depress the pedal when it wants more.

random behavior → reward → conditioned behavior → reward

It is by this same method that animal actors are trained to perform seemingly impossible tasks. A desired behavior, such as turning clockwise, is broken down into small steps, each step being rewarded as it appears: first a turn of a foot, then a turn of the head, then a half-turn of the whole body, etc. (Skinner, 1961).

Operant conditioning is used to shape behaviors of all kinds, consciously and unconsciously, in all walks of life. Behaviors that are preferable and therefore rewarded (positive response) are increased in frequency. Behaviors that are not desired, and therefore punished (negative response) reduce in frequency or disappear altogether. With humans, operant conditioning is a common mechanism for shaping the behavior of children, friends, colleagues, spouses—everyone. Once a behavior is shaped, the process that facilitated the shaped behavior falls from awareness (if it ever was in awareness), and the resulting shaped behavior remains as an implicit memory. Many behaviors and habits were first shaped by operant conditioning—learning to say "please" and "thank you," for example. Praise, pleasure, and contact will increase a behavior; disapproval, pain, and withdrawal will decrease it.

Traumatic incidents can shape behavior through operant conditioning. When this happens adapted responses to stress can develop. For example, a person's difficulty speaking in public may be traceable to a childhood where assertive speech elicited violent reprisal. When natural impulses for assertive speech become associated with punishment they are extinguished. If faced with a situation where public speaking is required—even at a business meeting—that individual might suffer an anxiety or panic attack with symptoms including racing heart, cold sweat, difficulty breathing, etc.

When a traumatic incident is repeated, as with physical abuse, domestic violence, incest, or torture, mental, emotional, and behavioral strategies for coping can become habituated, closing off the possibility of exercising other options, even in less stressful circumstances. Those who were molested or beaten as children or teenagers might later be vulnerable to sexual abuse or violence, because their natural impulses to protect themselves and protest (physical and verbal) were extinguished. Expectation of hurtful treatment by others or one's own failed capabilities can stubbornly persist despite overwhelming evidence that such is no longer the case. Behaviors and beliefs conditioned during traumatic events seem to have a greater enduring power than those conditioned under lesser degrees of stress. Even one instance of a failed or punished survival strategy during traumatic circumstances can be enough to extinguish that behavior from one's repertoire.

On a hopeful note, operant conditioning can also work in reverse. When strategies used to meet a traumatic threat are successful, they become more available and more likely to be used again. Sometimes this is called *stress inoculation*.

State-dependent Recall

State-dependent recall is another important phenomenon related to traumatic memory. When a current internal state replicates the internal state produced during a previous event, details, moods, information, and other states associated to that event may be spontaneously recalled or set in motion. This theory has often been applied to learning, predicting that information learned during specific states induced by various drugs or alcohol are better recalled under the same conditions, that is, under the influence of the same substance (Eich, 1980; Reus, Weingartner, & Post, 1979). A tasty example is provided by college students who have tried to use this phenomenon to advantage in the hopes of increasing their chances of passing exams. The strategy is to increase recall of the difficult material by eating chocolate while studying and then eating chocolate while taking the exams. It is not known, however, whether the success of this strategy (as reported by the students) is determined by the internal state elicited by the increased blood sugar, the stimulant in the cocoa, or the psychological associations of the chocolate. And, of course, it could just be a trumped-up excuse for indulgence by collegiate chocoholics.

State-dependent recall can also occur unbidden. It is not uncommon for a trauma to be recalled into awareness by an internal condition (increased heart rate or respiration, a particular emotional mood, etc.) that is reminiscent of the original response to the trauma. This process can be set in motion by a multitude of classically conditioned external triggers: a color, sight, taste, touch, smell, etc. It can also be incited by exercise, excitement, or sexual arousal. Anything that is a reminder of the trauma response is a possible catalyst.

It is also possible that state-dependent recall could be elicited under conditions that replicate body posture. This has not been discussed in the literature, but it is a logical extension of this theory and a ripe area for research. Feedback from postural proprioceptive nerves could have the same memory power as the proprioceptive nerves of internal sensations that must be involved in state-dependent recall under the influence of drugs or alcohol (see the next chapter for a discussion of proprioception). Asking a client to reconstruct his posture before and during a trauma will often bring details to awareness. However, such a technique must be used with caution, as it can easily stimulate more recall than the client is prepared to handle (see Chapter 5). Postural state-dependent recall can also be caused unwittingly, as, for example, when a physically abused child either freezes or screams when casually or inadvertently tossed over another's knee in play. (*Charlie's traumatic recall was triggered by the sensation of pressure on his right leg and his view of Ruff out of his right eye—replication of two conditions from the dog attack. State-dependent reminders of touch and sight set his reaction in motion.*)

Memory and PTSD

PTSD appears to be a disorder of memory gone awry. Individuals with PTSD cannot make sense of their symptoms in the context of the events they have endured. They are further plagued by state-dependent triggers and/or other classically conditioned associations to their traumas. Their traumatic experiences freefloat in time without an end or place in history.

An understanding of the somatic side of memory may provide clues to understanding the special memory features of PTS and PTSD. That is the topic of the next chapter.

CHAPTER THREE

The Body Remembers

Understanding Somatic Memory

Rhyme and Reason

There was an old woman who lived in a shoe,
She had so many children, she didn't know what to do.
But try as she would she could never detect
which was the cause and which the effect.

—Piet Hein

This chapter addresses two questions: What is meant by somatic memory? How can understanding this phenomenon be useful in the treatment of posttraumatic stress disorder and other trauma-related conditions? The implicit memory system is at the core of somatic memory. Individuals with PTSD suffer inundation of images, sensations, and behavioral impulses (implicit memory) disconnected from context, concepts, and understanding (explicit memory). Hopefully, greater understanding of somatic memory and implicit processes will help link implicit and the explicit memory systems (which will be further discussed in Chapter 8).

Somatic memory relies on the communication network of the body's nervous system. It is through the nervous system, via synapses, that information is transmitted between the brain and all points in the body. A basic understanding of its organization will help in understanding the phenomenon of somatic memory.

Three nervous system divisions are the most relevant with regard to trauma: the sensory, autonomic, and somatic. Each will be addressed separately, and

Figure 3.1. Organization of the central nervous system.

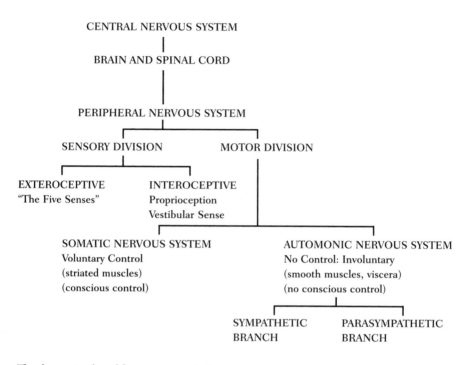

CENTRAL NERVOUS SYSTEM

BRAIN AND SPINAL CORD

PERIPHERAL NERVOUS SYSTEM

SENSORY DIVISION   MOTOR DIVISION

EXTEROCEPTIVE   **INTEROCEPTIVE**
"The Five Senses"   Proprioception
                            Vestibular Sense

SOMATIC NERVOUS SYSTEM   AUTOMONIC NERVOUS SYSTEM
Voluntary Control   No Control: Involuntary
(striated muscles)   (smooth muscles, viscera)
(conscious control)   (no conscious control)

                            SYMPATHETIC   PARASYMPATHETIC
                            BRANCH   BRANCH

This diagram is adapted from numerous similar ones.

then consolidated in the section on "Emotions and the Body." Figure 3.1 illustrates the organization of the body's central nervous system.

THE SENSORY ROOTS OF MEMORY

The sensory system has everything to do with memory. The nervous system transmits sensory information gathered from both the periphery and the interior of the body via synapses, through the brain's thalamus, on the way to the somatosensory area of the cerebral cortex of the brain. This is the first step of memory, the processing and encoding of information. Some of it will be stored for future reference and retrieved when pertinent. Much of it will never be stored and is quickly forgotten.

The sum total of experience, and therefore all memory, begins with sensory input. It is through the senses that one perceives the world. They provide continual feedback to the brain on the status of both internal and external environments. It is through the senses that reality takes form.

> *Take a minute to become aware of the mass of sensory information com-ing to and from your body right now. First notice your external environ-ment. You are standing, sitting, or lying on some kind of surface. Without looking at it, can you can identify if that surface is soft or hard, cold or warm? What sounds are your ears hearing? Is there enough light to eas-ily see the words on this page? Can you feel your hands holding this book? Notice how the cover and pages feel to your hands. Is the cover smooth or textured? Your external environment also includes how your clothes feel to your skin. Is your shirt smooth or scratchy? Slacks comfortable or too tight? Is the air temperature comfortable for the amount of clothing you have on?*
>
> *What about your internal environment? Without looking in a mirror, can you estimate the position of your shoulders, back, neck, and head? Where, and in which direction, are you tilted or twisted? Are you sitting up straight? Are you relaxed or tense? And notice that you shift position from time to time, even if only slightly. What are the sensations that cause you to change your posture to maintain comfort? Is your foot going to sleep or your neck beginning to ache? You might also notice if there is a taste in your mouth—sweet, sour, salt, smoke, bitter? Are there any smells that you are aware of? Soon you will probably become gradually preoc-cupied with additional internal bodily sensations that will tell you that you are hungry, thirsty, tired, restless, stiff, have a full bladder, etc.*

All of this input and more is constantly being transmitted to the brain all the time—whether consciously or not. Each of these cues, whether coming from the body's periphery or from inside the body, is a sensation.

Sensory Organization

There are two main sensory systems: *exteroceptive* and *interoceptive*. Exterocep-tors are nerves that receive and transmit information from the environment *out-side* of the body by way of the eyes, ears, tongue, nose, and skin. Interoceptors are nerves that receive and transmit information from the *inside* of the body, from the viscera, muscles, and connective tissue.

The Exteroceptive System

The exteroceptive system is the one with which you are likely to be the most familiar. It includes the sensory nerves that respond to stimuli emanating from outside of the body, that is, the external environment, via the basic five senses: sight, hearing, taste, smell, and touch. All exteroceptors are responsive to large and small changes in the external environment. An individual will usually have greater facility in one or another sense or heightened sensitivity to some kinds of stimuli. Individuals with damage to one of these senses (for example, the visually or hearing impaired) will often compensate for their deficit by developing greater acuity in one or more of the others. The visually impaired, for example, often have acutely sensitive hearing.

> *Which of the five senses are you most receptive to? What gets your attention? Do you become particularly alert when you hear a strange sound, smell a particular odor, or when something moves suddenly across your field of vision? Do you easily feel nuances of contact to the surface of your skin? Perhaps there is more than one, but you probably favor one over the others. Which of these senses is most active in your memories? Are you more likely to remember the taste of a meal, its smell, or how it looked? Are you more visual, auditory, or tactile? When you are alone, remembering your lover, do you have stronger images of his or her face, voice, or touch?*

The Interoceptive System

The interoceptive system is comprised of sensory nerves that respond to stimuli emanating from inside the body. There are two major types of interoception: *proprioception* and the *vestibular sense*. Proprioception is further comprised of the *kinesthetic* sense, which enables one to locate all the parts of his body in space, and the *internal* sense, which gives feedback on body states such as heart rate, respiration, internal temperature, muscular tension, and visceral discomfort. The vestibular sense helps the body sustain a balanced posture and maintain a comfortable relationship with gravity.

The Kinesthetic Sense

It is the kinesthetic sense that enables you to bring the tip of your finger to touch the tip of your own nose when your eyes are closed. This small task, familiar as a sobriety test, is an amazing feat. Those who doubt it should sit beside a friend, and try to touch the *friend's* nose while his own eyes are closed. Successful nose targeting relies on input from muscles and skeletal connective tissue that indicate the height and angle of one's arm, hand, and finger. It also requires an internal sensory schema for where all parts of one's body are located, to register just where the nose is. When aiming to touch *another's* nose there is access to the former, but not the latter. The kinesthetic sense also makes walking possible by indicating where legs and feet are located at any given point in time. It is the kinesthetic sense that makes it possible to learn and execute all sorts of motor tasks and behaviors.

The importance of the kinesthetic sense can best be illustrated by an example of its loss. The *APA Monitor* (Azar, 1998) reported the fascinating case of a man who, as the result of a viral infection, had lost the kinesthetic part of his proprioceptive sense, as well as his sense of touch. Though all of his motor functions were intact, without looking the man had not the least notion of the position of his body; he could not even stand. Eventually he was able to compensate to some degree for his loss. Through years of trial and error, he learned to move and walk relatively normally, bring a glass to mouth, etc., relying on his sense of sight to provide the cues that used to come from his kinesthetic nerves. However, if when he was standing the lights went out and he was deprived of visual cues, he would crumple to the floor and be unable to rise until someone turned on the lights. Without vision to help him, he had no idea how to place a hand palm down on the floor, raise his elbow over his hand at the angle necessary to get enough leverage to push himself up, etc. In addition, without vision he could not tell where or how to place his feet under him or shift his weight properly for support and to get his balance. Access to implicit memory of simple, usually automatic movements and procedures was lost to him. Such cases are exceedingly rare, but their study is useful in helping us understand how necessary the senses are to everyday living.

The kinesthetic sense is central to implicit, procedural memory. It helps one learn and then to remember how to do something. It keeps track of where to put and how to move hands, fingers, feet, and trunk to replicate, for example, walking, bike riding, skiing, typing, handwriting, or dancing. Active in our waking hours, the kinesthetic sense functions automatically. Though it is usually unconscious, you can increase your awareness of the kinesthetic sense.

> *Close your eyes and see how accurately you can describe your current body position. Notice, for example, the angle of your right arm. Is the palm of your hand facing up or down? Is your left foot turned out or in? In which direction is your head tilted? You can also try having a friend "sculpt" your body into a different position and see if you can tell exactly where and how each limb has been placed. Next time you sit down to write or eat—something which is normally an automatic procedure for you, stored in implicit memory—try doing it differently. Hold the pen or fork in a different way or in the opposite hand. Can you now just write or eat without thinking about what you are doing? Most likely you will not be able to. If such a behavior is not stored in implicit memory, success will depend upon conscious effort.*

The Internal Sense

It is the internal sense that registers the state of the body's internal environment: heart rate, respiration, pain, internal temperature, visceral sensations, and muscle tension. "Butterflies" or an ache in the stomach is a familiar internal sensation. A "gut feeling" is a summation of the internal sense. It is the internal sense that helps to identify and name our emotions. Each basic emotion—fear, anger, shame, sadness, interest, frustration, or happiness—has an accompanying set of discrete body sensations, stimulated by patterned activity in the brain. This biology of emotion in the body and brain is called affect.

> *Can you feel how fast your heart is beating without taking your pulse? Can you feel your breathing—where and how deep? Where in your body are you feeling tense or relaxed right now? Try again to eat or write with the opposite hand. Notice your visceral reactions and any changes in muscular tension. Do you feel discomfort anywhere? Is there a change in the tension of your arm or shoulders? That is your internal sense alerting you to a change in normal procedure. Then change back to write or eat in the way that is normal for you and notice if there is a corresponding*

relaxation of the internal alert. Remember the last time you were embar-
rassed. Did your face get hot? How about when you are angry; do your
shoulders get tense?

The internal sense is the foundation for neurologist Antonio Damasio's theory of somatic markers. He proposes that the experience of emotions is comprised of body sensations that are elicited in response to various stimuli. Those sensations, and their related emotions, become encoded and then stored as implicit memories associated with the stimuli that originally evoked them (classical conditioning). Memory of the emotions and sensations can later be triggered into recall when similar stimuli are present, though their origin will not always be remembered (Damasio, 1994). For example, if someone eats something and becomes ill, the next time she sees, smells, or is offered that same food she may feel some degree of nausea. After a time the strong reaction will likely fade, but she may continue to have an automatic aversion to that food, perhaps even forgetting the origin of her dislike, "Oh, no thank you. I never eat that. I just don't like it!" Damasio's somatic marker theory will be further discussed in the last section of this chapter.

The Vestibular Sense

The vestibular sense indicates when one is in an upright position in relationship to the earth's gravity. Centered in the inner ear it may, when disturbed, cause bouts of dizziness or vertigo, motion sickness, or loss of balance. People particularly attuned to this sense may feel all the nuances of motion. For example, during an airplane flight such a person will notice each slight turn and tip of the plane that others register only when looking out of the window.

Many amusement parks have an attraction that tricks the usually cooperative relationship between sight and the vestibular sense. The Haunted Shack at Knotts Berry Farm in Southern California is one example. When one walks through this stationary building it is impossible to keep one's balance. It is necessary to hold onto railings to avoid falling. The guides say it is because the house is built over a site where the earth's gravity is different, though they have no trouble negotiating the place themselves—standing at an angle. The secret of such attractions is that a seemingly normal structure is actually built at an angle. The floor, roof, and walls slant 20 or 30 degrees. The tables, chairs, pictures, etc., are also placed at the same slant and nailed in place. With eyes open, the normal person will rely on visual cues to determine the direction of gravity. In this instance, that causes a bit of chaos. One tries to get straight with what one sees. However, with closed eyes the vestibular sense will kick in, telling which way is up. The guides follow the vestibular information, which is why they stand on a slant—but, of course it is never suggested that the guests try that, as it would spoil the secret.

Somatic Memory and the Senses

Each of the senses discussed above is germane to the discussion of the somatic basis of memory in general and traumatic memory in particular. Our first impressions of an experience usually come from our senses—both interoceptive and exteroceptive. These impressions are not encoded as words, but as the somatic sensations they are: smells, sights, sounds, touches, tastes, movement, position, behavioral sequences, visceral reactions.

Memory of an event stored in implicit memory as sensations can sometimes be elicited if similar sensory input is replicated (state-dependent recall). There are many examples of this from normal daily life. Just about everyone has at one time or another experienced state-dependent sensory-based memory recall triggered by a song, taste, or smell: "Oh my gosh, I hadn't thought about that in years!" Sometimes it is something positive, sometimes negative, but it happens all the time.

Sensory Memory and Trauma

Sensory memory is central to understanding how the memory of traumatic events is laid down—how, as Bessel van der Kolk (1994) would put it, "The Body Keeps the Score." Memories of traumatic events can be encoded just like other memories, both explicitly and implicitly. Typically, however, individuals with PTS and PTSD are missing the explicit information necessary to make sense of their distressing somatic symptoms—body sensations—many of which are implicit memories of trauma. Which information is missing varies: for some it will be a specific fact or facts that have been forgotten; for others it may be a key, the "aha!" that puts the facts at hand together into something meaningful. One of the goals of trauma therapy is to help those individuals to understand their bodily sensations. They must first feel and identify them on the body level. Then they must use language to name and describe them, narrating what meaning the sensations have for them in their current life. At times, though not always, it then becomes possible to clarify the relationship of the sensations to past trauma.

One of the difficulties of PTSD is the phenomenon of *flashbacks*, which involve highly disturbing replays of implicit sensory memories of traumatic events sometimes with explicit recall, sometimes without. The sensations that accompany them are so intense that the suffering individual is unable to distinguish the current reality from the past. It *feels like* it is happening now. (Chapter 6 includes tools to help clients use sensory awareness to distinguish the reality of the moment from memories of a past reality. Chapter 8 includes a protocol for stopping a flashback.)

A flashback can be triggered through either or both exteroceptive and interoceptive systems. It might be something seen, heard, tasted, or smelled that serves as the reminder and sets the flashback in motion. It can just as easily be a sensation arising from inside the body. Sensory messages from muscles and connective tissue that remember a particular position, action, or intention can be the source of a trigger. It is not uncommon, for example, for a woman who has been raped to be just fine making love with her husband except in the position that is reminiscent of the rape. Even an internal state aroused during a traumatic event, for example, accelerated heart rate, can be a trigger. For that reason, some individuals with PTSD do not do well with aerobic exercise. The accelerated heart rate and increased respiration can be implicit reminders of the accelerated heart rate and increased respiration that accompanied the terror of their trauma. Accelerated heart rate caused by stimulants in coffee, tea, cola, or dark chocolate can also be problematic for some. These are all examples of triggers elicited through state-dependent recall. The following case excerpt (continued from p. 4) will illustrate.

CHARLIE AND THE DOG, PART II

Charlie summoned my attention in the most restricted of voices. I turned to see him sitting on a cushion on the floor at my right, stricken. His body was totally rigid—arms pinned to his sides, legs stretched out in front—and he could barely speak. Ruff was calmly lying beside him with her head on Charlie's knee. He managed to squeak out, "I am very distressed right now. I am terribly afraid of dogs." I asked if he could move Ruff away, or move away himself, but I could see that was not possible. Charlie was literally, and visibly, frozen stiff (tonic immobility). With the help of a group member, I managed to get Ruff to move away from Charlie. But he remained frozen in place. Later, following therapeutic intervention (which will be described in Chapter 8), as we talked about what had just occurred, Charlie was convinced that Ruff had had her mouth on his thigh where he had previously been bitten, not on his knee. In fact, he was astounded to learn that Ruff had just laid her head on his knee. Charlie's reaction was set in motion by exteroceptive stimuli of touch and sight. Ruff's contact with Charlie's right leg, combined with a glimpse from his right peripheral visual field, had been reminiscent enough of his previous traumatic encounter to trigger Charlie's traumatized condition. His body instantly remembered the attack.

This example illustrates state-dependent recall brought about by specific, state-related conditions. Amazingly, Charlie was a regular at this retreat center and had encountered Ruff many times previously without incident, though he avoided her. He had never been triggered on previous occasions because the right combination of stimuli had never before occurred.

THE AUTONOMIC NERVOUS SYSTEM: HYPERAROUSAL AND THE REFLEXES OF FIGHT, FLIGHT, AND FREEZE

The limbic system of the brain could be called "survival central." It responds to extreme stress/trauma/threat by setting the HPA axis in motion, releasing hormones that tell the body to prepare for defensive action. The hypothalamus activates the sympathetic branch (SNS) of the autonomic nervous system (ANS), provoking it into a state of heightened arousal that readies the body for fight or flight. As epinephrine and norepinephrine are released, respiration and heart rate quicken, the skin pales as the blood flows away from its surface to the muscles, and the body prepares for quick movement. When neither fight nor flight is perceived as possible, the limbic system commands the *simultaneous* heightened arousal of the parasympathetic branch (PNS) of the

ANS, and tonic immobility (sometimes called "freezing")—like a mouse going dead (slack) or a frog or bird becoming paralyzed (stiff)—will result (Gallup & Maser 1977). As mentioned previously, it is not yet known what is happening in the HPA axis that causes the body to freeze instead of fight or flee.

In the case of PTSD, cortisol secretion is not adequate to halt the alarm response. The brain persists in responding as if under stress/trauma/threat. At this time it is not known which is the first driving factor: a continued perception of threat in the mind or insufficient cortisol. The result, however, is the same: The limbic system continues to command the hypothalmus to activate the ANS, persisting in preparing the body for fight/flight or going dead, even though the actual traumatic event has ended—perhaps years ago. People with PTSD live with a chronic state of ANS activation—hyperarousal—in their bodies, leading to physical symptoms that are the basis of anxiety, panic, weakness, exhaustion, muscle stiffness, concentration problems, and sleep disturbance.

It is a vicious cycle, first set in motion in the service of survival, but enduring as impairment. During a traumatic event the brain alerts the body to a threat. In PTSD, the brain persists in calling and recalling the same alert, stimulating the ANS for defensive reactions of fight, flight, or freeze. The once protective reactions of heightened pulse, paled skin, cold sweat, etc., so necessary for defense, evolve into the distressing symptoms of disability. With Pavlov's dog, an originally neutral stimulus (the bell) became associated with and capable of eliciting a normal physiological response to food (salivation). With PTSD the same thing happens. Objects, sounds, colors, movements, etc., that might otherwise be insignificant neutral stimuli become associated through classical conditioning to the traumatic incident, causing traumatic hyperarousal. These stimuli then become external triggers that are experienced internally as danger. Confusion can result when recognition of external safety doesn't coincide with the inner experience of threat. Symptoms can become chronic or can be triggered acutely. Breaking this cycle is an important step in the treatment of PTSD.

Under normal circumstances, the PNS and SNS branches of the ANS function in balance with each other (see Table 3.1). The SNS is primarily aroused in states of stress, both positive and negative. The PNS is primarily aroused in states of rest and relaxation, pleasure, sexual arousal, and others. Both branches are always engaged; however, one is usually more activated, the

Table 3.1. Autonomic nervous system (smooth muscles, involuntary).

SYMPATHETIC BRANCH	PARASYMPATHETIC BRANCH
Activates during positive and negative stress states, including: sexual climax, rage, desperation, terror, anxiety/panic, trauma	States of activation include: rest and relaxation, sexual arousal, happiness, anger, grief, sadness
Noticeable signs	**Noticeable signs**
Faster respiration Quicker heart rate (pulse) Increased blood pressure Pupils dilate Pale skin color Increased sweating Skin cold (possibly clammy) Digestion (and peristalsis) decreases	Slower, deeper respiration Slower heart rate (pulse) Decreased blood pressure Pupils constrict Flushed skin color Skin dry (usually warm) to touch Digestion (and peristalsis) increases
During actual traumatic event OR with flashback (visual, auditory and/or sensory)	**During actual traumatic event OR with flashback (visual, auditory and/or sensory)**
Preparation for quick movement, leading to possible fight reflex or flight reflex	Can also activate concurrently with, while masking, sympathetic activation leading to tonic immobility: freezing reflex (like a mouse, caught by a cat, going dead). Marked by simultaneous signs of high sympathetic and parasympathetic activation.

other suppressed—like the dipping and rising arms of a scale. When one side is up, the other is down. In other words, under normal circumstances they constantly swing in complementary balance to each other (Bloch, 1985). The following scenario illustrates the interactive balance of the SNS and PNS:

You are sleeping peacefully; the PNS is active and the SNS suppressed. Then you awaken and find you set the clock wrong and are already one hour late for work. The SNS shoots up; your heart rate accelerates, you are instantly awake. You move quickly—showering, dressing, then leaping into your car and gunning it to get you down the road. When you get to the first corner you notice the clock on the church tower and realize this was the weekend that winter time started and the clocks have turned back one hour; actually, you are not late after all. The SNS decreases and the PNS rises. Your heart rate slows; you breathe more easily and continue your journey more relaxed. However, when you get to work, you find you double

scheduled your first appointment time and have two irate clients to deal
with. The SNS again accelerates, suppressing the PNS. . . .

So it goes throughout the average day, with the SNS and PNS swaying in balance with each other to meet the variety of stresses and demands typical of daily life. However, something very different happens under the most extreme form of stress, traumatic stress. First the limbic system commands the SNS to prepare the body to fight or flee. But if that is not possible—there is not time, strength, and/or stamina to succeed—the limbic system commands the body to freeze.

The most commonly observed instance of freezing is the mouse that "goes dead" when caught by a cat. That image is useful to many with PTSD who have frozen in the face of mortal threat, as they can relate to the mouse's dilemma as well as its physiological response. Instinctively, a mouse will flee if its limbic system estimates it can get away. As with all animals facing threat, the SNS activates drastically in order to meet the demand for fight or (in this case) flight. If, however, the mouse becomes trapped, or if during its attempt to flee, the cat nabs it, the mouse will "go dead." It will lose muscle tone, like a rag doll. According to Gordon Gallup (1977) and Peter Levine (1992, 1997), the likely mechanism underlying this hypotonic response, *tonic immobility*, is an unusual imbalance in the ANS. In this extreme circumstance the SNS will remain activated, while the PNS simultaneously becomes highly activated, masking the SNS activity, causing the mouse to "go dead." This has several evolutionary purposes, including relying on the likelihood that the cat will lose interest (felines will not eat dead meat unless they are starving), affording the possibility of escape. Analgesia is also an important function of tonic immobility, numbing the body and the mind. If the cat does eat the mouse, in its deadened state the pain and horror of death will be greatly diminished (Gallup & Maser, 1977; Levine, 1992, 1997).

Something similar appears to happen with humans when mortally threatened. Interviews with people who have fallen from great heights, or been mauled by animals and survived, reveal that they tend to go into a kind of altered state where they feel no fear or pain. Rape is another prime example. It is typical for the victim of rape, at some point, to become literally unable to resist. The body goes limp, and many report being in an altered state during that time. Many victims of rape suffer from dreadful shame and guilt because of it. It is infuriating to continue to hear of rape cases being thrown out of court because the victim had not fought back. "Going dead" and being unable to fight back are frequent reactions to physical violence such as rape and torture (Suarez & Gallup, 1979). How one reflexively/instinctively responds to a life-threatening situation depends on many factors, including one's own instincts and one's physical and psychological resources. Bruce Perry and colleagues (1995) have theorized that men respond more often to threat with fight and flight, and women and children more often with going dead or freezing. Their theory makes sense, as men often have more physical resources—constitutionally greater strength, speed, and agility—than women and children. Additionally, this could be due to learned behavior, as men and women are conditioned to respond differently to threat. This is another area ripe for research. (*Charlie fainted when he was attacked. Whether fainting is a form of tonic immobility is not known at this time, but it is a likely consequence of an overwhelmed ANS.*)

Understanding the funtioning of the ANS helps in explaining the vulnerability to stress of those with PTSD. PTSD is characterized, in part, by chronic ANS hyperarousal. The system is always stressed. A person with a normal balance in the ANS will be able to swing with rises and falls of arousal. When a new stress comes along the arousal in the SNS moves from little or no arousal to higher arousal and then back again when the stress is dealt with. For those with PTSD the picture is different: When SNS arousal is constantly high, adding a new stress shoots it up even higher; it is easy to go over the top, causing them to feel overwhelmed. This difficulty is familiar to many with PTSD who wonder why they cannot handle daily stress like everyone else or like they used to be able to.

THE SOMATIC NERVOUS SYSTEM:
MUSCLES, MOVEMENT, AND KINESTHETIC MEMORY

The somatic nervous system (SomNS) is responsible for voluntary movement executed through the contraction of skeletal muscles. Understanding the function of the SomNS is pertinent to grasping the mechanism by which traumatic events can be remembered implicitly through the encoding of posture and movement.

Basically, the only thing a muscle can do actively is contract. That is it. A muscle contracts when it receives an impulse through the nerve that serves it.

Impulses for contraction of visceral muscles are primarily transmitted through nerves of the autonomic nervous system (ANS); impulses for contraction of skeletal muscles are carried through nerves of the SomNS. As long as a muscle continues to receive neural impulses, it continues to be contracted. When lifting a heavy object, for example, several muscles are stimulated to contract, remaining contracted until the object is released. Muscle tension is an active process comprised of chronic muscle contraction. Relaxation, usually thought of as an active process, "Hey, just relax," is actually a passive state. It is the absence of neural impulses, noncontraction.

To move any part of the body in any way, in any direction, it is necessary to contract at least one skeletal muscle.

> *Look at the palm of your left hand. Try to separate your left little finger from the other fingers of that hand without moving the rest of your hand or other fingers.*

That little movement is accomplished by a neural impulse, sparked by the words in the previous sentence. The impulse is transmitted from the brain along the ulnar nerve and causes contraction of the muscle *abductor digiti minimi* of the left hand, causing the little finger to move away from the other fingers. When the finger is not purposefully moving to the side, it will come back toward the other fingers. That lesser movement is actually caused by the noncontraction (relaxation) of the abductor digiti minimi.

Most physical movement is much more complex, accomplished through multiple, simultaneous, and/or consecutive muscle contractions and non-contractions.

> *Next try to move your right index finger to touch your nose in slow motion.*

That simple movement is actually made up of several muscle contractions—some consecutive, some simultaneous—and noncontractions. Specific muscles are being stimulated to contract in order to point the finger, close the hand, turn the hand, bend the elbow, and raise the arm. At the same time, there are other muscles that must remain noncontracted (relaxed) in order for the arm to bend and permit the movement of the elbow away from the body. All of these elements are necessary to accomplish what appears to be the single, simple movement of touching index finger to nose. It is the SomNS that commands the movement and the kinesthetic sense that assures its accuracy.

It is through the SomNS that behaviors, movements, and physical procedures are performed. It is via interoceptive, proprioceptive nerves that they are perceived. For a movement to be encoded and recorded as implicit memory, both nerve sets are necessary. The somatic nerves cause a movement, the interoceptive nerves give you the feeling of it. It is the interoceptive system that helps you know that you are making the correct movement, especially when you are not observing what you are doing.

For a new procedure, movement, or behavior to be maintained in memory, proprioceptive nerves from muscles, tendons, and skeletal connective tissue— ligaments and fascia—relay information on position, posture, and action via afferent nerves to the brain. For an old procedure, movement, or behavior to be recalled into use, those same schemata need to be activated and then relayed via efferent nerves, through the SomNS and proprioceptive system, out to the appropriate muscles and connective tissues. The SomNS will cause the contraction of the muscles necessary to accomplish the movement. The proprioceptive nerves will give feedback on the correctness of the movement.

When a new behavioral sequence is learned, images associated with that learning experience (positive or negative) may be stored simultaneously. When that same behavioral sequence is repeated, those images are sometimes also recalled.

> *Have you ever taught a child to tie a shoe? I did last year and I remember it as being a bit exasperating. As I'd been tying my own shoes for many, many years, it was totally automatic. It took me several minutes to think of just how I do it, and a while longer to be able to communicate the maneuver to my young friend. I endeavored to simply describe what for my fingers became automatic long ago. Once I had a feel for the procedure, I had to further slow it down and break it up into microsteps that the child could follow. For years, without thinking about it, each hand "knew" which lace to take, which way to turn one over the other, etc. It was a great challenge to resolutely think about what I was*

doing and, furthermore, explain it. I sometimes became confused and, while in the midst of it all, I had flashes of remembering my father teaching me to tie my shoes in this same way. Were those images triggered by the situation, the theme, the replicated movements, or a combination of all of these elements? Eventually, I was able to competently explain and demonstrate the procedure in slow motion. My young friend watched with great interest and attempted to duplicate my every move. But for her, of course, it was something new and she tried many times before getting it right once, several more to get it right consistently. She had to concentrate intensely on what her fingers were doing each step of the way. By the next week she had it down pat. That experience gave me pause: I wonder if she will recall some of these images of me teaching her when as an adult she engages in the behavior of teaching a child to tie his laces in the same way? Will replicating these same movements bring me to mind?

Trauma, Defense, and the Somatic Nervous System

The autonomic nervous system, among other things, directs blood flow away from viscera and skin to the muscles for the duration of fight, flight, and freezing responses. The somatic nervous system directs the musculature to carry out that response. Without quick and powerful movements of muscles controlled by it, there would be no fight and there would be no flight. The freezing—tonic immobility—state would also be impossible without its action.

Defensive behavior can be instinctual or learned through instruction or conditioning. Even usually instinctual defensive reflexes must sometimes be taught. Some infants born prematurely will lack, for example, the falling reflex. Many can then be taught to reach out hands and arms to catch their falls. In such a circumstance the specific neural impulses must be trained to respond automatically to the cue of falling.

Other types of training can go a long way to prepare individuals to meet certain kinds of stressful or traumatic incidents, raising self-confidence. For example, many women and men who have been assaulted or raped have benefited from self-defense training, which reawakens normal fight responses and teaches additional protective strategies. Self-defense training is accomplished through repeatedly practicing defensive movements, building synaptic patterns that will repeat spontaneously under threat.

Safety in schools and on the job also depends on the creation of automatic reactions and behaviors. Fire, earthquake, and other types of drills prevent panic through rehearsal of precise behaviors (where to go and what to do) and sometimes of specific movements (dive under the desk).

Operant conditioning plays a role here, too. Fight, flight, and freeze responses are not just instinctual behaviors; they are subject to influence—positive and negative—according to how successful or unsuccessful they have been in actual use. When a defensive behavior is successful, it becomes recorded as effective; the chance of the same behavior being used in a future threatening situation increases. Likewise, when a defensive behavior fails, the chance of repeating it decreases. For example, if a boy is harassed by a group of bullies and is successful in defending himself, later as an adult, he will be more likely to strike a defensive posture when threatened. If, however, he is overpowered by the bullies and, furthermore, goes into tonic immobility, when threatened as an adult he will be more likely to freeze. A behavior does not always require repetition to be encoded and stored. Behaviors associated with traumatic incidents can be instantly stored via the SomNS. In some cases it takes only one traumatic incident where defensive behavior was either impossible or unsuccessful for it to be wiped from an individual's protective repertoire. (*See Daniel's case on p. 89 for an example of applying behavioral repetition as a resource in the therapy session. The conclusion of Charlie's therapy on p. 171 also illustrates this principle.*)

Traumatic Memory Recall and the Somatic Nervous System

You were just in your living room and wanted something. You come into the kitchen and . . . "What was it I came in here for?" You scratch your head. You swear. You can't remember. You wrack your brain. You go back to the spot where the intention originated, assuming the same sitting posture you were in at that moment—BINGO! "Now I remember!"

That recall strategy doesn't always work, but it does often enough that many use it. What is it about resuming a particular body posture, one held at the time an idea is germinated, that aids in memory recall? The above example is a useful application of the concept of state-dependent recall. As previously mentioned, the theory of state-dependent recall holds that if you return to the state you were in at the time a piece of information was encoded, you can retrieve that same piece of information. Though usually discussed in reference to internal states, state-dependent recall is exceedingly relevant to postural states.

State-dependent recall can sometimes be triggered through the SomNS by inadvertently (or purposely) assuming a posture inherent in a traumatic situation. When used purposefully, it can aid the possibility of memory recall and/or reestablishment of behavioral resources. Reconstructing the movements involved in a fall or a car accident can often accomplish this. However, when state-dependent recall hits unexpectedly, it can cause chaos:

A mid-thirties woman sought therapy for panic that developed while making love with her husband. Her arm had accidentally gotten caught under her in an awkward position, firing off memories of a rape she thought she had long put behind her. The rapist had pinned the same arm under her in the same position.

Often, the movements caused by the SomNS can be used to intentionally facilitate state-dependent recall. Following nuances of movement can also be useful. The following case illustrates how focusing on a seemingly trival movement has the potential to catalyze a trauma therapy.

Carla's 3-year-old daughter had died four years ago. Carla had become fixated on the horror of the illness and was unable to speak of her child's death and process the meaning of her loss. During one therapy session, Carla mentioned one of the medical consultations; she remembered it as being particularly difficult, but couldn't recall why. As she spoke, I saw that Carla's head was making slight jerking movements to her right. I brought this to her attention. She had not been aware of it, but noticed it now that I mentioned it. I encouraged her to let the movement develop if she could. Slowly the movement became bigger, becoming an obvious turn of the head to the right. When her head made its full turn, Carla began to cry. Now Carla remembered. At that consultation, she sat facing the doctor, but to her right was the illuminated x-ray that told the tale of her daughter's fate; she had not been able to look at it. It was at that consultation that Carla first knew her daughter would not be able to survive. Making this connection was an important step in helping Carla to move past the horror of the diagnosis to the grief of her loss.

The SomNS has many roles in the experience of trauma. It carries out the trauma defensive responses of fight, flight, and freeze through simple and complex combinations of muscular contractions that result in specific positions, movements, and behaviors. In cooperation with proprioception, the SomNS is also party to encoding traumatic experiences in the brain. Somatic memory recall can occur when those same positions, movements, and behaviors are replicated either purposefully or inadvertently.

EMOTIONS AND THE BODY

Emotions, though interpreted and named by the mind, are integrally an experience of the body. Each emotion looks different to the observer and has a different bodily expression. Every emotion is characterized by a discrete pattern of skeletal muscle contraction visible on the face and in body posture (somatic nervous system). Each emotion also *feels* different on the inside of the body. Different patterns of visceral muscle contractions are discernible as body sensations (the internal sense). Those sensations are then transmitted to the brain through the proprioceptive nerves. How an emotion looks on the outside of the body, in facial expression and posture, communicates it to others in our environment. How an emotion feels on the inside of the body communicates it to the self. To a large extent, each emotion is the result of interplay between the sensory, autonomic, and somatic nervous systems interpreted within the brain's cortex.

The English language is a bit awkward when it comes to differentiating the conscious experience of emotions from body sensations. The word "feeling" usually stands for both: I *feel* sad and I *feel* a lump in my throat. Perhaps it is no accident that "feel" stands for both experiences, a semantic recognition that emotions are comprised of body sensations. A possible way out of the confusion, though, might be to distinguish between feelings, emotions, and affects. Donald Nathanson (1992) addresses this dilemma. He distinguishes affect as the biological aspect of emotion, and feeling as the conscious experience. Memory, he suggests, is necessary to create an emotion, while affects and feelings can exist without memory of a prior experience.

That emotions are connected in some way to the body should come as no surprise. Everyday speech is full of phrases—in many languages—that reflect the link of emotion and body, psyche and soma. Here are a few examples from American English:

> *Anger*—He's a pain in the neck.
>
> *Sadness*—I'm all choked up.
>
> *Disgust*—She makes me sick.
>
> *Happiness*—I could burst!
>
> *Fear*—I have butterflies in my stomach.
>
> *Shame*—I can't look you in the eye.

There is also commonality in physical sensation of emotion—how an emotion feels in the body:

> *Anger*—muscular tension, particularly in jaw and shoulders
>
> *Sadness*—wet eyes, "lump" in the throat
>
> *Disgust*—nausea
>
> *Happiness*—deep breathing, sighing
>
> *Fear*—racing heart, trembling
>
> *Shame*—rising heat, particularly in the face

And typical physical behaviors that go with each emotion:

> *Anger*—yelling, fighting
>
> *Sadness*—crying
>
> *Disgust*—turning away
>
> *Happiness*—laughing
>
> *Fear*—flight, shaking
>
> *Shame*—hiding

And, of course, many facial and postural expressions of emotion are easily recognized (though some are much more subtle) by the observer:

Anger—clamped jaw, reddened neck

Sadness—flowing tears, reddened eyes

Disgust—wrinkled nose with raised upper lip

Happiness—(some kinds of) smile, bright eyes

Fear—wide eyes with lifted brows, trembling, blanching

Shame—blushing, averted gaze

Emotions are expressed from the first moments of life outside of the womb. The typical wail of the newborn as it exhales its first breath could be interpreted as a first expression of emotion. The newborn is limited in its emotional repertoire. At first it is only able to distinguish between discomfort and comfort, wailing in response to the former, calm in response to the latter. During the first weeks of life, distinct emotions are of limited range. Quickly, though, the baby's collection increases, differentiating nuances within the ranges of discomfort and comfort.

There are several theoretical models of emotion. What to call individual affects is subject to debate, though most models include some form of "anger," "sadness," "fear," "disgust," "happiness," and "shame" among their lists. Certainly how an individual names his own emotions is subject to variation, depending on how emotions were labeled by her family and culture. In this chapter, though, our concern is not with what an emotion is called. What is pertinent to this part of the discussion of trauma and the body is how an emotion is sensed and expressed.

A Select History of the Emotion-Body Connection

Charles Darwin's Cross-cultural Survey

Charles Darwin was the first scientist to systematically investigate the universality of emotion and the somatic features of emotional expression in man. In 1867 he surveyed an international group of missionaries and others who were living around the world in different cultures: Aboriginal, Indian, African, Native

American, Chinese, Malayan, and Ceylonese. He asked specific questions in order to find out if types of emotions, as well as their observable expressions, were consistent throughout different cultures. He discovered that not only was there great commonality to all ranges of emotion across unrelated and often isolated cultures, but there was also commonality to the somatic expression of those emotions (Darwin, 1872/1965). When reviewing Darwin's work, one can have little doubt that emotions and the body go hand in hand the world over.

Tomkins's Affect Theory

Silvan Tomkins's affect theory was born simultaneously with his first child. As he witnessed this momentous event he was drawn to the infant's emotional outburst, amazed at the similarity of expression between the infant's cry and an adult's. From this impetus his study broadened to encompass identifying the similarity of emotional expression across generations. He was most interested in categorizing each identified affect by physical expression, noting not just the facial characteristics of each, but also changes in body posture. Donald Nathanson (1992) has taken Tomkins's theories several steps further.

Joseph LeDoux's Emotional Brain

Joseph LeDoux's theories on the relationship of the body and emotions are well known and highly respected. He recognizes the interdependence of brain and body, as well as the bodily expressions of emotion. The evolutionary function of emotions, he believes, are associated with survival—both with regard to dealing with hostile environments, and in furthering the species through procreation (LeDoux, 1996).

Antonio Damasio's Somatic Marker Theory

Neurologist Antonio Damasio has worked with and studied individuals with damage to regions of the brain having to do with emotion. He has discovered that emotion is necessary to rational thought. Further, he found that body sensations cue awareness of the emotions. Damasio (1994) concludes that to be able to make a rational decision, one has to be able to feel the consequences of that decision. Just projecting a cognitive judgment is not enough; it is the *feel* of it that counts.

According to Damasio, an emotion is a conglomerate of sensations that are experienced in differing degrees, positive and negative. They make up what he calls *somatic markers,* which are used to help guide decision-making. That is, body sensations underlie emotions and are the basis for weighing consequences, deciding direction, and identifying preferences.

The most recognizable example of the function of somatic markers are the kinds of choices people make everyday based on "gut feelings."

The Somatic Basis of Emotion

The following four-part exercise is intended to offer a firsthand experience of what is meant by the somatic basis of emotion.

> *First, take a minute to survey the sensations of your body right now. Notice your breathing—where and how deep. What is your skin temperature—is it consistent all over? Check your heart rate—either subjectively or by taking your pulse. Check out the position of your shoulders—are they raised, fallen, hunched? Are they tense or relaxed? Notice the sensations in your gut—relaxed, tense, butterflies, hungry, etc. Lastly, notice if you are moving or twisting or tilting your body or any body part in a particular way.*
>
> *Second, think about the emotion of anger. Remember, the last time you were angry. Can you bring forth any of that feeling? What were you angry about and who were you angry with? What did you say and/or think? Are there any remnants of that emotion? Again survey your breathing, skin temperature, heart rate, shoulder position and tension, stomach sensations. Also notice your position, posture, or behavior. Has anything changed from your first survey: autonomic signs, muscle tension, movement?*
>
> *Third, remember a time you felt happy and safe. Where were you? What were you wearing? Who were you with? Bring up the scene with as much visual, auditory, and sensory imagery as you can muster. What do you feel in your body? Has it changed from when you were feeling angry? Is your muscle tension the same? How about your heart rate? Are you smiling?*
>
> *Fourth, remember a time you felt afraid. Do not pick your worst traumatic event, but something with a small amount of fear. What was it that*

scared you? When you remember it now, what happens in your body? Are you breathing differently? Has your heart rate changed? Have muscles become tense or flaccid? What is the temperature of your hands and feet?

Before ending the experiment, return to the memory of when you felt happy and safe. Bring back the imagery of the place, activity, and others who were present. Now what do you sense in your body?

Emotions and Trauma

Anger/Rage

Anger is an emotion of self-protection. It may involve an effort to prevent injury or specify a boundary. It is also a common response to having been threatened, hurt, or scared, or to the person who caused it. Anger can escalate to rage when the threat is extreme or when assertions of "Don't!" or "Stop!" are not respected. When anger or rage become chronic in the wake of trauma, difficulties can emerge in an individual's daily life. Inappropriate or misdirected anger can interfere with interpersonal relationships and job stability; provoking others to anger can become a danger in itself. How many instances of "road rage," for example, are incited by a short temper that has its roots in unresolved trauma?

Anxiety/Fear/Terror

Fear alerts one to danger or potential harm. Both fear and anxiety are common emotions for those with PTS and PTSD. LeDoux (1996) distinguishes between the two: Fear, he believes, is stimulated by something in the environment; anxiety is stimulated within the self. LeDoux also sees fear as the driving force in several psychological disorders: phobias, anxiety and panic disorders, and obsessive-compulsive disorders.

Terror is the most extreme form of fear. It is central to the experience of trauma, the result of the (perception of) threat to life. The biology of terror involves the HPA axis and sympathetic nervous system arousal discussed previously in this chapter. Once the trauma is over, terror usually reduces to fear, even for those suffering its aftermath. However, during a flashback, terror can return in all of its original intensity.

One of the problems for individuals with PTS and PTSD is that fear persists long after the threat abates, frequently associating to more and more aspects of their environment. The fear they once felt to an external threat becomes anxiety generated from within. As discussed earlier, this might be caused by insufficient cortisol production, or it could be caused by a continued perception of threat. Whatever the cause, the result is debilitating. When fear is so broadly generalized, its protective function becomes handicapped. When everything is perceived as dangerous, there is no discrimination of what truly is dangerous. It is like a burglar alarm that's ringing all the time. You never know when it is ringing for real. It is typical for those with PTSD to repeatedly fall prey to dangerous situations. Their internal alarm systems are so overloaded that they have become disabled. One result of trauma therapy is the reestablishment of the protective function of fear.

Shame—Disappointment in the Self

Shame is a difficult emotion to deal with in any context. This is no less true for shame that arises as the result of trauma. Individuals with PTSD often have a large component of shame involved in the disorder. Shame is expected to be a component of PTSD when the trauma is the result of sexual abuse or rape. It is less expected under other circumstances. Why, then, is shame such a common feature of other trauma constellations? In almost any unresolved trauma there will be the question of "Why couldn't I stop that (do more, fight back, run away, etc.)?" It is possible that individuals with PTSD believe on some deep level that they have let themselves (and perhaps others) down and/or that something integral is wrong with them that they fell victim to the trauma. Of course, shame is not the only driving force in PTSD, but it may be an important one.

One of the difficulties with shame is that it does not seem to be expressed and released in the same way as other feelings: Sadness and grief are released through crying, anger through yelling and stomping about, fear through screaming and shaking. What, then, can be done to alleviate shame when it does not discharge, abreact, or cathart? Acceptance and contact appear to be keys to relieving shame. Though it appears not to discharge, it does seem to dissipate under very special circumstances—the nonjudgmental, accepting contact of another human being.

When considering shame, it can be important to look at both of its sides.

Usually shame is perceived as a terrible emotion, because it is so awful to feel. Who wants to feel shame? However, shame, like every other affect has a survival value. Fear, for example, warns of danger, while anger tells the other not to take one step (literally or figuratively) closer. What, then, is the survival value of shame? It appears that shame, at least through evolution, has served to keep an individual's behavior in line with cultural norms that further "survival of the tribe." It socializes. Shame is an accepted component of socialization in many cultures. It is an emotion that has been elicited for thousands of years when a person's behavior has threatened not only himself, but also his whole group. Shame is one element that stops us from behaving in ways that might hurt us, our families, and our communities. It may, in fact, be the emotion that underlies the formation of a conscience. As an affect, shame is not all bad. It is common knowledge that acceptance is the first step in resolving any unwanted emotional state, and seeing shame as having a positive function might assist in achieving that step.

Grief

Grief is a response to loss or change. It is a great resource in the treatment of trauma and PTSD. By its nature, grief is a sign that an experience has been relegated to the past. It is usually a positive sign when a trauma client reaches the stage where grief arises. Sometimes a client will fear that his grief is a regression into trauma, but it is usually just the opposite, a healing progression. When working with body awareness, most clients will notice that their grief helps them to feel more solid, less fearful, if more sad. Grief usually emerges at various steps along the way in trauma therapy when an aspect of the trauma is resolved and the internal experience changes from present to past: "I *was* really scared," "That *was* really bad," etc. In this context grief is a sign that healing is taking place.

Integrating vs. Disintegrating Emotional Expression—A Proposal

Catharsis and *abreaction* are often used interchangeably to describe expression of emotions in the therapeutic setting. Catharsis actually refers to the cleansing power of emotions when disturbing memories are brought forth into consciousness. Abreaction is the emotional discharge that often accompanies catharsis. Regardless of what one calls these emotional eruptions, care must be taken, especially with trauma clients.

There is an ongoing professional debate as to the usefulness of abreaction in the treatment of PTSD. When a client is crying or expressing anger, it is not always easy to tell if such emoting is helping or making matters worse. The question usually debated is whether or not abreaction should be allowed or encouraged at all. However, the relevant question is: When does abreaction help and when does it not?

This debate points the way to an important area for research: how to distinguish integrating from disintegrating abreaction. Is it possible that observation of autonomic nervous system (ANS) arousal could hold a key to distinguishing these two ranges of emotional expression during trauma therapy—the one that appears to be therapeutic and integrating and the other that might be disintegrating and possibly retraumatizing?

It is possible that therapeutic abreaction can be recognized by hallmarks of primarily parasympathetic arousal: The skin has color, respiration is deep with emotional sounds coming on the exhale. Disintegrating abreaction, on the other hand, might be revealed to have hallmarks of primarily sympathetic arousal: The skin is pale, sometimes clammy, respiration is rapid, sometimes jerky, emotional sounds come mostly on the inhale. Observing the ANS to differentiate types of abreaction could greatly facilitate and simplify the therapeutic process.

CHAPTER FOUR

Expressions of Trauma Not Yet Remembered

Dissociation and Flashbacks

Traumatic dissociation and *traumatic flashbacks* are the two most salient features of PTSD. Both are at the root of its most distressing psychological and somatic symptoms. As mentioned before, dissociation might be a constant factor in every case of PTSD. Some form of flashback might also be a constant. These two aspects of PTSD often occur in tandem; it is not possible to have traumatic flashbacks without some form of traumatic dissociation also being operable, though dissociation can occur without flashbacks.

As mentioned before, dissociation implies a splitting of awareness. During a traumatic incident, the victim may separate elements of the experience, effectively reducing the impact of the incident. The process of dissociation involves a partial or total separation of aspects of the traumatic experience—both narrative components of facts and sequence and also physiological and psychological reactions. Amnesia of varying degrees is the most familiar kind of dissociation, but there are others. One person might become anesthetized and feel no pain. Another might cut off feeling emotions. Someone else might lose consciousness or feel as if he had become disembodied. The most extreme form of dissociation happens when whole personalities become separated from consciousness (dissociative identity disorder). Later those same reactions and/or others may still be operational. One might continue to become anesthesized when under stress, be unable to access emotions, or feel disembodied when anxious.

A flashback is a reexperiencing of the traumatic event in part or in its entirety. Most familiar are visual and auditory flashbacks, but the term flashback might also apply to somatic symptoms that replicate the traumatic event in some way. Whatever the sensory system involved, a flashback is highly distressing, because it feels as though the trauma is continuing or happening all over again.

In people with PTS and PTSD, traumatic event(s) are remembered differently than nontraumatic events. They are not yet actually "remembered" in the normal sense. Usually, "memory" implies the relegation of an event into one's history—a position on one's lifeline. Memory puts an experience into the past, "I remember when . . ." With PTS and PTSD traumatic memories become dissociated, freefloating in time. They pounce into the present unbidden in the form of flashbacks.

DISSOCIATION AND THE BODY

The term *dissociation* has been within the psychological lexicon for over one hundred and fifty years. It was first coined by Moreau de Tours in 1845 (van der Hart & Friedman, 1989) as an attempt to understand hysteria. The concept was further developed by Pierre Janet beginning in 1887 with his article, "Systematized Anesthesia and the Psychological Phenomenon of Dissociation." Janet could be called the "father of dissociation," as it is his work in this area that laid the foundation for current theories. He hypothesized that consciousness was comprised of varying levels, some of which could be held outside of awareness. In the latter part of the twentieth century, Janet's work was rediscovered and applied to modern theories of dissociation and PTSD (van der Hart & Friedman, 1989; van der Kolk, Brown, & van der Hart, 1989).

Even though the concept has been in use for a long time, how dissociation occurs is not yet known, though there is plenty of speculation. It appears to be a neurobiological phenomenon that occurs under extreme stress. Whether it is an attempt by body and mind to dampen trauma's impact or a secondary result of trauma is unknown. It is possible that dissociation is the mind's attempt to flee when flight is not possible (Loewenstein, 1993).

Individuals who report dissociative phenomena during traumatic incidents express it as: "It was like I left my body." "Time slowed down." "I went dead and could not feel any pain." "All I could see was the gun, nothing else mattered." After an event the victim can still feel dissociated, continuing to feel "beside oneself" long after the event is over. In Sue Grafton's (1990), *"G" is for*

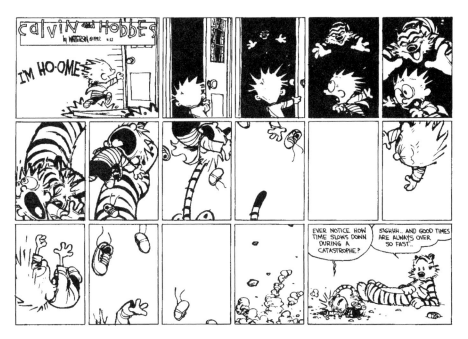

Calvin and Hobbes ©1992 Watterson. Reprinted with permission of Universal Press Syndicate. All rights reserved.

Gumshoe, protagonist Kinsey Millhone describes dissociation a few hours after she was nearly shot as, "My soul's not back in my body yet."

Following a traumatic event, dissociative phenomena can continue for years or even arise for the first time years later. They may be identified by numbing, flashbacks, depersonalization, partial or complete amnesia, out-of-body experiences, inability to feel emotion, unexplained "irrational" behaviors, and emotional reactions that seemingly have no basis in reality. It is likely that some form of dissociation is fueling every case of PTS and PTSD.

The SIBAM Model of Dissociation

Peter Levine's SIBAM dissociation model is most useful for conceptualizing dissociation. It is based upon the supposition that any experience is comprised of several elements. Complete memory of an experience involves integrated recall of all of the elements. SIBAM is the acronym for: *S*ensation, *I*mage, *B*ehavior, *A*ffect, and *M*eaning (Levine, 1992). These are the elements of experience identified by Levine. He postulates that elements of highly distressing/traumatic experiences can be dissociated from one another. This postulation is based on the premise that less distressing experiences remain intact in memory. A simple example of a complete experience can be found in the memory of last night's dinner:

> I had a Mexican meal. Right now I can still feel the bite of the chilis in my mouth (sensation). I can visualize my plate with the variety of colors (image). There is more saliva in my mouth and a urge to swallow (behavior). I feel content and peaceful as I remember the pleasant meal (affect). And it was a relaxing break from my work (meaning).

Memories associated with a greater degree of stress can also be remembered fully.

When Karen was about 6 she fell from a tree swing. When as an adult she described the incident during a therapy session, she remembered she was pushed from behind: "I can feel the hands on my back side and the drop feeling in my stomach from the swish of the swing (sensation). I can see the ground below as I swing, and then the sky above after I fell (image). I feel a little anxious, and then angry as I remember (affect) and I stop breathing so deeply (behavior). I remember feeling I was out of control because the girl pushing me wouldn't stop (meaning)."

Levine proposes that during some episodes of traumatic stress elements of the experience become disconnected. An individual with PTS or PTSD might later report a disturbing visual memory (image) and a strong emotion connected to it (affect), but cannot make any sense of it (dissociated meaning); a child might exhibit repetitive play after a disturbing event (behavior), but doesn't display any emotion (dissociated affect) or appear to remember it at all (image).

One shortcoming of the SIBAM model is that there is no mechanism for distinguishing traumatic dissociation from simple forgetting. Of course, forgetting might be just the result of an experience not being significant enough to encode fully or at all into long-term memory.

Returning to the concept of memory systems, understanding dissociation in the context of the SIBAM model becomes easier. Implicit memory involves sensory images, body sensations, emotions, and automatic behaviors. Explicit

Figure 4.1. A sampling of relationships of dissociated SIBAM elements with specific trauma reactions. The dark lines indicate which elements are associated; the lighter lines, which elements are dissociated.

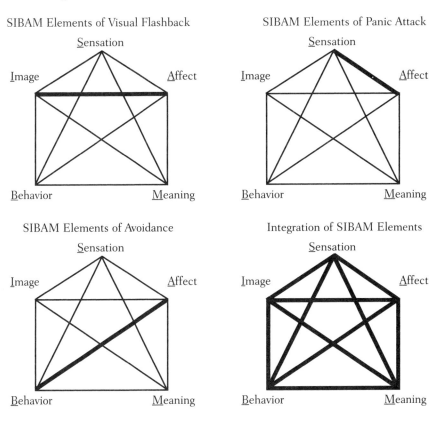

memory involves the facts, sequence, and resolution (meaning). Dissociation can appear in many forms, as varying combinations of elements are dissociated. And of course, unless there is complete amnesia, when some elements are dissociated others are associated. In Figure 4.1, possible pairings are proposed for understanding three symptoms of PTSD.

Clients with anxiety and panic attacks may talk persistently about disturbing physical sensations and resulting fear (affect). It may be difficult or impossible for them to identify what they heard or saw that triggered the anxiety (image), what they need to do to reduce the anxiety (behavior), or what the fear actually stems from (meaning). Clients trapped in visual flashbacks will shuttle between the images and terror, blocked in their ability to feel their body in the present (sensation), move in a way that would break the spell (behavior), or put the memory into context (meaning). The SIBAM model can be an effective tool for helping to identify which elements of an experience are associated and which are dissociated. Once identified, missing elements can be carefully assisted back into consciousness when the client is ready. (*Charlie remembered most of the attack; he had visual images of it. He was very aware of his body sensations and emotions, and he knew what it meant to him. However, he was missing at least two salient pieces. One was an additional aspect of meaning: being able to discriminate the dog who attacked him from other dogs. The other was a protective behavioral strategy that he could engage to protect himself. See Chapter 8 for a description of how those elements were finally integrated.*)

FLASHBACKS

The term *flashback* was popularized in the 1960s to describe disturbing sensory experiences reported by individuals who had used the drug LSD. Following use of the drug—days, weeks, even years later—some of them reexperienced aspects of their most frightening hallucinogenic "trips."

Traumatic flashbacks are quite similar. They can occur while awake or in the form of nightmares that disrupt sleep. One client called them "having nightmares while I am awake." Traumatic flashbacks are comprised of sensory experiences of terrible events replayed with such realism and intensity that they are difficult to distinguish from in-the-moment reality.

Flashbacks that are primarily visual and/or auditory are the type most commonly identified. They are easily recognized, as the individual can usually describe what he is seeing or hearing. Less familiar are flashbacks that are primarily emotional, behavioral, and/or somatic. Instances of hyperarousal, hyper-startle reflex, otherwise unexplainable emotional upset, physical pain, or intense irritation may all be easily explained by the phenomenon of flashback. Lindy, Green, and Grace (1992) reported on sensory and behavioral flashbacks, describing what they termed "somatic reenactment" of traumatic events. One woman's recurring somatic and behavioral flashback involved a persistent, debilitating symptom of urinary urgency that caused her repeated, unnecessary trips to the restroom. Both symptom and behavior developed following a restaurant fire where her life was literally spared by an empty bladder; her friends had died, trapped in the restroom. She had not needed to join them and escaped with her life. "Mrs. F's symptom repetitively captured the moment when she, sensing no pressure on her bladder, chose not to join her friends while they, sensing full bladders, went to their deaths" (Lindy et al., 1992, p. 182). This example poignantly illustrates how someone can act in ways that seem to make no sense unless you know the trauma history. However, the nature of somatic reenactment becomes clear when the missing pieces of information are supplied. It is possible that certain unexplainable physical symptoms that puzzle doctors and plague patients may be incidents of somatic reenactment.

Behavioral flashbacks are quite common, though not often recognized as such. Young children, for example, are apt to act out their traumatic experiences rather than verbalizing them. Which types of behavior are flashbacks is sometimes not clear. For example, is the child who molests or physically harms another youngster being aggressive, or is he reenacting what was done to him? This is another area worthy of scientific research.

Flashbacks and the Brain

Flashbacks can be varied. They can involve the recall of implicit memory of a traumatic event in the absence of explicit memory, so that the references necessary to make sense of the memory or to put it in perspective are lacking. They can also involve explicit memory of the sequence (including scenes) of the whole or parts of the event. Flashbacks almost always include the emotional and sensory aspects of the traumatic experience; that is why they are so disturbing. This implies that the amygdala is part and parcel of the flashback process. At the same time, it appears that the contextual features typical of hippocampal processing are absent, which would be consistent with theories indicating hippocampal suppression during trauma and trauma recall (Nadel & Jacobs, 1996; van der Kolk, 1994, among others). In addition, flashbacks are usually set in motion through either classically conditioned or state-dependent triggers. That would imply that the whole nervous system is involved in the phenomenon. Three examples:

Roger was in his early twenties when as a rookie policeman he shot and killed a suspect for the first time. He froze as he watched blood flow from the man's chest.

He kept yelling, "I'm sorry. Why'd you make me do that?" He seemed to recover and handle the situation well until two years later when he was the first officer on the scene where a man had been shot during a brawl. The next officer to arrive found Roger yelling those same words, apparently confusing the two situations.

With Roger it is clear that a visual cue, blood flowing from a dead man's chest, triggered his flashback. He was horrified to have killed someone. When at first he could not reconcile what had happened, he just forgot about it and it *seemed* not to bother him anymore. Obviously that was not the case.

Marie was 29 when her daughter, Tanya, turned 5. On the first day of kinder-garten, Marie went into a panic and would not let Tanya go to school. Marie kept Tanya home for several weeks, panicking each morning when she should have dropped her off at school. The rest of the day, Maria was fine. Finally her husband convinced her to seek treatment. Maria had reacted without knowing why. It was only during psychotherapy that she recalled being molested at the same age in her kindergarten. Newspaper archives confirmed that a teacher's aide had been con-victed of molesting several of the children.

Marcy suffered chronic bladder infections as a child. She was subject to many forms of invasive treatments in an effort to cure her condition. As she grew up, though she always remembered having the infections, she had no memory of the doctor visits. Shortly after she was married she suffered a bout of cystitis—not uncommon for a new bride. During the doctor's examination, she became so hyperaroused that she broke into a cold sweat and became panicked. She was unable to tell the doctor what she was feeling and she proceeded to faint.

Marcy's sensory flashback was triggered by sensation and posture. It was only later that she was able to connect her reaction to her earlier treatments. They had clearly been more distressing than she had remembered.

Summary

Understanding the phenomenon of flashbacks is one of the best ways to con-solidate the theory that has been presented in Part I. Flashbacks are com-prised of dissociated, implicitly stored information that becomes elicited under state-dependent conditions. They can be triggered by interoceptive or exteroceptive sensory cues, and are expressed through hyperarousal of the autonomic nervous system as well as behaviors directed by the somatic nervous system.

In Part II, principles and techniques for stopping and preventing flashbacks, as well as other trauma-related symptoms, will be presented.

PART TWO

Practice

CHAPTER FIVE

First, Do No Harm

Timing Toast

There's an art of knowing when.
Never try to guess.
Toast until it smokes and then
twenty seconds less.

— Piet Hein

M ost psychotherapists know all too well just how tricky trauma therapy
can be—regardless of the theory or techniques that are being applied.
The risk of a client's becoming overwhelmed, decompensating, having anxiety
and panic attacks, flashbacks, or worse, retraumatization, always lingers.
Reports of clients' getting such overwhelming flashbacks during therapy sessions that the treatment room is misinterpreted as the site of the trauma and
the therapist perceived as the perpetrator of the trauma are common. It is also
not unusual for clients to become unable to function normally in their daily
lives during a course of trauma therapy—some even requiring hospitalization.
Working with trauma seems, universally, to be rather more precarious than
other areas of psychotherapy. We talk about the dangers, but we do not usually write about them.

The dangers inherent in the therapeutic treatment of trauma are not news
even though posttraumatic stress disorder (PTSD) did not appear as an offi-
cial diagnosis until the publication of *DSM-III* in 1980. In 1932, psychoana-
lyst Sándor Ferenczi presented a courageous paper before the 12th
International Psychoanalytical Congress in Wiesbaden. In it he admitted to

his colleagues that psychoanalysis could be retraumatizing: "some of my patients caused me a great deal of worry and embarrassment . . . [they] began to suffer from nocturnal attacks of anxiety, even from severe nightmares, and the analytic session degenerated time and again into an attack of anxiety hysteria" (Ferenczi, 1949, p. 225). He acknowledged that the usual way to explain such phenomena among his colleagues had been to blame the patient for having "too forceful resistance or that he suffered from such severe repressions that abreaction and emergence into consciousness could only occur piecemeal." But he dug deeper, "I had to give free rein to self-criticism. I started to listen to my patients. . . ." He went on to speculate that both premature interpretations, and unspoken countertransference feelings could lead to an undermining of the therapeutic process, including patient decompensation to the point of "hallucinatory repetitions of traumatic experiences" (Ferenczi, 1949).

In a more recent but equally courageous paper, "Relieving or Reliving Childhood Trauma?" Onno van der Hart and Kathy Steele (1997) remind us that directly addressing traumatic memories is not always helpful and can sometimes be damaging to our clients. They propose that those clients who are not able to tolerate memory-oriented trauma treatment may still benefit from therapy geared to relieve symptoms, increase coping skills, and improve daily functioning.

Just what is going wrong when trauma therapy becomes traumatizing? A client is most at risk for becoming overwhelmed, possibly retraumatized, as a result of treatment when the therapy process accelerates faster than he can contain. This often happens when more memories are pressed or elicited into consciousness—images, facts, and/or body sensations—than can be integrated at one time. The major indicator of overly accelerated therapy is that it produces more arousal in the client's autonomic nervous system (ANS) than he has the physical and psychological resources to handle. It is like an automobile speeding out of control, the driver unable to find and/or apply the brakes.

ON BRAKING AND ACCELERATING

I've taught several friends to drive. The lessons always took place in my car. I sat in the passenger seat with no dual controls. Being a bit worried about my own safety as well as that of my student and my car, I always began the same way. First, before my driving student was allowed to cause the car to move forward, I taught her how to stop, how to brake.

My driving student was drilled in shifting her foot to the brake pedal repeatedly until the movement was automatic, accurate, and performed confidently without looking. Only when my student (and I) were secure in her ability to find the brake pedal and stop the car reflexively did I deem it safe for her to use the gas pedal and learn to (slowly) accelerate, while periodically returning to the brake pedal—stop and go. The more confident my student became in handling the car and braking appropriately, the more acceleration (within the bounds of the speed limit) she could dare.

Safe driving involves timely and careful braking combined with acceleration at the rate that the traffic, driver, and vehicle can bear. So does safe trauma therapy. It is inadvisable for a therapist to accelerate trauma processes in clients or for a client to accelerate toward his own trauma, until each first knows how to *hit the brakes*—that is, to slow down and/or stop the trauma process—and can do so reliably, thoroughly, and confidently (Rothschild, 1999).

Why Brake, Slow Down, or Stop the Therapy Process?

The symptoms of PTSD are depleting. Typically, the client with PTSD alternates periods of frenetic energy and periods of exhaustion. Sometimes the therapy process is difficult because the client just doesn't have the reserves necessary to focus, confront, and resolve the issues at hand. Reducing hyperarousal both in the therapy session and in the client's daily life will not only give the client much needed relief but also enable him to rest more effectively. This, in turn, will give him a greater capacity and resources to face his traumatic past.

A useful analogy is to liken the person with PTSD to a pressure cooker. The unresolved trauma creates a tremendous amount of pressure both in the body and in the mind in the form of ANS hyperarousal. With a modern pressure cooker, once the pressure is built up, it becomes impossible to open it, but if you could it would explode. You must first slowly relieve the pressure, a little "pft" at a time. Then, and only then, can you open any pressure cooker safely.

The same applies to PTS and PTSD. If you try to open the client up to trauma while the pressure is extreme, you risk explosion—which in a client's case can mean decompensation, breakdown, serious illness, or suicide. However, with judicious application of the brakes to gradually *relieve* the pressure, the whole process of trauma therapy becomes less risky. Each client should be evaluated on an individual basis. Some require more liberal braking than others. Optimally, the pace of the therapy should be no slower than necessary, but no quicker than the client can tolerate while maintaining daily functioning.

EVALUATION AND ASSESSMENT

Determining which type of trauma and which type of trauma client you are dealing with will go a long way in helping to determine the treatment plan. Lenore Terr (1994) has distinguished two types of trauma victims, *Type I* and *Type II*. She originally made this distinction with regard to children. Type I refers to those who have experienced a single traumatic event. Type II refers to those who have been repeatedly traumatized.

Terr's typing system is quite applicable to adults, though further designation is useful. Two subtypes of Terr's Type II traumatized individuals should be distinguished: *Type IIA* are individuals with multiple traumas who have stable backgrounds that have imbued them with sufficient resources to be able to separate the individual traumatic events one from the other. This type of client can speak about a single trauma at a time and can, therefore, address one at a time. *Type IIB* individuals are so overwhelmed with multiple traumas that they are unable to separate one traumatic event from the other. The Type IIB client begins talking about one trauma but quickly finds links to others—often the list goes on and on.

Type IIB clients can also be divided into two categories. The Type IIB(R) is someone with a stable background, but with a complexity of traumatic experiences so overwhelming that she could no longer maintain her resilience. Typical of this type of client are the Holocaust survivors described in the aforementioned Norwegian study by Malt and Weisaeth (1989). Type IIB(nR) is someone who never developed resources for resilience, as described by Schore (1996).

One of the reasons for evaluating the client's trauma type is that each has different therapeutic needs, especially with regard to the therapeutic relationship and transference. Usually, Type I and Type IIA individuals require less attention to the therapeutic relationship and develop a less intense transference to the therapist. Many have already internalized the resources that might be offered within the framework of a long-term, transference-focused relationship. This is not to say that transference issues will not arise; however, with this kind of individual, the therapeutic relationship is in the background and their need to work on specific traumatic memories is the foreground. After the initial interview and assessment, Type I and Type IIA clients can usually move quickly to working directly with the traumatic incident(s) that brought them to therapy.

For Type IIB clients, on the other hand, resource (re)building through the therapeutic relationship will be a prerequisite to directly addressing traumatic memories. With the Type IIB(R), the therapeutic relationship will help reacquaint the client with resources she knew but has lost touch with due to the complex and overwhelming nature of the traumas she has endured. With the Type IIB(nR) client, the therapeutic relationship may be the whole of the therapy, building resources and resilience that were never developed. The special needs of both categories of Type IIB clients will be further discussed in the following section on the therapeutic relationship.

There is an additional type of client that is worthy of mention when discussing trauma clients. This is the client who has many symptoms of PTSD but reports no identifying event(s) that qualify him for that diagnosis. Scott and Stradling (1994) proposed an additional diagnostic category they call prolonged duress stress disorder (PDSD). Chronic, prolonged stress during the developmental years (from neglect, chronic illness, a dysfunctional family system, etc.) can take its toll on the autonomic nervous system, just short of pushing it to the point of fight, flight, or freeze. The needs of this type of client often resemble those of the Type IIB(nR) client. When they do, the most helpful treatment method may also be the same. In both instances, the therapeutic relationship has the potential to infuse many of the coping skills and resilience that may have been missed during development.

THE ROLE OF THE THERAPEUTIC RELATIONSHIP
IN TRAUMA THERAPY

There can be a tendency for a trauma therapy to be focused more on individual traumatic incidents than on the overall impact a trauma has on the client's interpersonal relationships, including the therapy relationship. For some clients that bias is beneficial; for others it can be detrimental. It is important to address, at least briefly, the role of the therapeutic relationship in trauma therapy in order to stress the individual needs of trauma clients.

In addition, the body does figure significantly in work with the therapeutic relationship, as attention to it while focusing on the therapist-client interaction can be very informative. Observing signs of autonomic nervous system arousal, patterns of tension, and intentional movements (Levine's [1992] name for slight muscle contractions that may indicate a behavioral intention that has not been fulfilled) may provide insight into the impact of the relationship between therapist and client. With some trauma clients, the trauma is reenacted in the transference—sometimes as psychological symptoms (i.e., mistrust), sometimes as somatic symptoms (as with the case example on p. 141).

Schore (1996) suggests that experiences in the therapeutic relationship are encoded primarily as implicit memory, often effecting change within the synaptic connections of that memory system with regard to bonding and attachment. Attention to the therapeutic relationship will, with some clients, help to transform negative implicit memories of relationships by creating a new encoding of a positive experience of attachment. When this is successful, the client internalizes a new representation of a caring relationship in both mind and body. This does not change the client's past, but will give him a new somatic marker (Damasio, 1994) when he thinks of relationships or anticipates entering into one(s) in the future. When successful, the positive attachment to the therapist can change habituated avoidance or fear of interpersonal relationships into desire for healthy contacts.

The Therapeutic Relationship: Foreground or Background?

It is generally accepted that the therapeutic relationship is critical to the outcome of any psychotherapy. This is no less so in trauma therapy; however, it will be of varying importance. Direct work with traumatic memories should not begin until the therapeutic relationship is secure for the client and the client feels safe with the therapist. Many clients will move through this stage fairly quickly, sometimes even by the second or third session. Others will require several sessions before they feel safe with the therapist and the therapy process. For those clients the principles and tools outlined in future chapters will aid in preparing them for the difficulties of delving into their traumatic memories with the models of trauma therapy favored by their therapists.

There are also a good number of trauma clients for whom developing safety within the therapeutic relationship will take a very long time. In some cases, working on feeling secure in that relationship may in fact be a large portion of the therapy, pushing direct work with trauma to the sidelines. The building of resources outlined in the next two chapters will be important for such clients: body awareness, braking, muscle toning, resource building, boundaries, dual awareness, etc. Trauma issues will not be avoided, though they cannot be addressed directly. Instead, much of the traumatic material will arise within the interaction between the therapist and the client. When that happens, trauma is addressed through the transference the client develops to the therapist as well as the therapist's own countertransference reactions. This type of trauma therapy is often arduous. However, it can be very rewarding when both therapist and client are willing and able to see it to completion.

What distinguishes these types of trauma clients? Why is the therapeutic relationship a more critical aspect of their therapy? What happens if the therapist misjudges and directly addresses trauma prematurely with this kind of client?

It is the Type IIB trauma client for whom the therapeutic relationship will be most urgent. Included in this category is what Judith Herman (1992) calls complex PTSD. As discussed above, these clients have suffered such massive and/or multiple trauma that they lack the resources and resilience necessary for any direct confrontation of traumatic memories to be constructive. A betrayal of trust appears to figure in the overall picture of these clients. Many clients in this group have suffered at the hands of others in some way, either through neglect in their developing years or human-caused victimization at any age (abuse, assault, rape, incest, war, torture, domestic violence, etc.). The earlier this has occurred in life, the greater the damage to the ability to trust other humans. When victimization occurs later in life, betrayal of previously developed trust is the larger issue. In some cases developmental deficits (neglect or other bonding failures) may also be a factor. As discussed in Chapter 2, failures of attachment can contribute to an individual's vulnerability to developing PTSD or other disorders (Schore, 1996).

With clients who have suffered interpersonal trauma, addressing trust issues in the therapeutic relationship increases in importance. The client who has never been able to trust another will need a chance to build it. The individual whose trust has been betrayed will need the chance to reestablish it. Both processes take time. Without trust, traumatic memories cannot be constructively confronted.

Not until trust in the therapist is established does the client have an ally with whom to confront his traumas. If traumatic memories are addressed directly before this trust has been developed, the client will be in the unfortunate situation of confronting his traumas (often again) in isolation. Under that condition, not only is the trauma not resolved, but it also can be made considerably worse.

Affect and Pain Regulation

While Allan Schore (1994) does not ponder the issue of trust directly, his massive work in the area of early bonding and attachment holds many clues to building trust with the Type IIB trauma client. Schore asserts that bonding between caretaker and infant is necessary for the child to develop the capacity to regulate its own emotions. He suggests that this capacity grows through the interaction of the child and the caretaker over time and has three critical phases: attunement, misattunement, and reattunement (Schore, 1994). Basically, the child and caretaker interact in face-to-face contact. As this proceeds at tolerable levels for the infant, it remains in contact (attunement). When the arousal level goes too high—either because of excitement or because of anger or disapproval on the part of the caretaker—the infant breaks contact (misattunement). When the infant's level of arousal reduces again to a tolerable range, it reestablishes contact with the caretaker—usually at a higher level of arousal than was previously tolerated before (reattunement) (Schore, 1994). This type of interaction forms the basis of attachment and may be critical to increasing the child's (and later the adult's) capacity to regulate stress, emotion, and pain.

When 6-year-old Tony fell and gashed her leg it hurt very much. In addition, she was very frightened as she was wheeled into the emergency room to be stitched up and her mother was told to stay outside. Tony became hysterical. Finally, the doctor allowed her mother to stand in the doorway of the emergency room, where Tony could see her. Tony vividly recalls how both her terror and her pain reduced dramatically at the sight of her mother. As the doctor worked on her leg, Tony kept her eyes riveted on her mother's.

Implications for the therapeutic relationship are many. Most therapists are familiar with its affect-regulating function. Unstable clients will often, for periods of time, seek out the therapist when upset, calming or crying with relief as they first catch sight of the therapist in the waiting room or at the sound of the therapist's voice on the telephone. There are a number of clients who are soothed between sessions just by hearing the therapist's outgoing voicemail message.

Attunement, Misattunement, and Reattunement

There is a conundrum with some Type IIB trauma clients. Trust in the therapist may grow following a conflict (a perception or suspicion of betrayal or other type of disruption), provided it is followed by repair of the relationship—misattunement and reattunement. When conflict risk is high, it can be a good idea to prepare the client for periods of perceived injury or betrayal by the therapist. Actual planning for such occurrences can go a long way toward turning them into constructive events.

Frank had never in his life had someone to depend on but himself. Both of his parents had been alcoholics, his father violent. Frank was fiercely independent and feared intimacy. He was also unstable emotionally. He had trouble keeping a job, as he was prone to emotional outbursts.

The first stage of therapy was aimed at increasing his stability. Resource building (see the next chapter), both physical and psychological, figured strongly in our early work together. Locating interpersonal resources, however was difficult. Frank's level of trust in anyone was very low. From the start I believed Frank to be a good candidate for premature therapy termination due to a conflict (misattunement). I waited, however, to broach the subject until we had developed a bit of a relationship. During an early therapy session I discussed with Frank the likelihood that later in the therapy he might become so angry with me that he would want to quit. He agreed that was possible; it had, in fact, been a problem with three previous therapists. I discussed Schore's concepts of attunement, misattunement, and reattunement with Frank, explaining that misattunement was not only predictable but desirable. Without it there was no opportunity for reattunement, which was necessary to strengthen the relationship. What, I asked, had he needed at those times when he could not resolve his anger with the earlier therapists? He claimed that his previous therapists had abdicated any responsibility for his feelings, that they had been unwilling to see what they had actually done and, most importantly, apologize. Discussing this with Frank before the fact gave me many insights into his personality, as well as the psychological injuries he had suffered. He was able to further reveal that the pain of his father's violence had paled when compared to his lack of remorse. Frank had never received an apology for his father's violent behavior.

A few weeks later, when I had to reschedule an appointment due to illness, Frank became furious and felt abandoned. He canceled his next appointment, leaving a message on my voicemail that he would call me if and when he wanted another. Because we had previously set the stage, I was in a good position to make contact with him and remind him of the earlier prediction. I suggested that he come in at least once for us to discuss what had happened. He agreed, but he was still very angry. In the session he ranted for a long time. When he seemed well vented, I ventured an apology for not being available when he needed me. He was skeptical and required reassurance that I really meant what I said and wasn't just apologizing because of what he had told me earlier. When I explained that I could see and hear the pain underneath his anger and felt genuinely sorry to not have been there for him, he began to cry. When he recovered he was able to accept my apology and our work together continued. That was our first, but far from our last, experience with misattunement and reattunement.

Another type of misattunement can occur when the client transfers the memory of a perpetrator onto the therapist and becomes afraid in her presence. When this occurs, the therapist must help the client to reality test and separate the two. This type of transference is not conducive to trauma therapy, as the client needs the therapist as an ally. Leaving a client to stew in this type of transferential misattunement can be very detrimental to the therapy process and can reinforce in the client a fear that nobody is safe.

As one can see, there are many routes to trauma treatment. The therapeutic relationship is of more and less importance to trauma therapy depending on the individual needs of the client. Evaluating the client's type as well as current level of functioning will help determine how much emphasis to give to the relationship.

SAFETY

In the Client's Life

The first rule of any trauma therapy is safety (Herman, 1992). That applies not only within the therapy setting, but also in the client's life. It is not possible to resolve trauma when a client lives in an unsafe and/or traumatizing environment. Resolving trauma implies releasing the defenses that have helped to contain it. If one is still living in an unsafe or traumatic situation, this will not be possible or advisable. When that is the case, helping the client to be and/or feel safe must be the first step. Much of this is common sense. For example: a battered wife must be safely separated from the violent husband; a client who was assaulted in his home might need to install extra door and window locks; a rape victim may need to await dealing with the memory of the rape until the rapist is adjudicated and imprisoned, etc.

Another strategy for increasing safety in the client's life is to identify and (temporarily) remove as many triggers as reasonably possible. Sometimes clients will protest removing triggers. They usually insist that they need to learn to live with their fears. However, sometimes they need the relief that comes with removal of a trigger to be able to later tolerate living with it. Temporarily removing a trigger will sometimes reduce or eliminate its effect and it can be returned to the client's life with little or no consequence.

Rodney frequently suffered episodes of depersonalization He literally lost the sense of his own skin, a very frightening experience. I suggested that he might regain it with the aid of a cool shower (the temperature differential might bring back the sensation of the periphery of his body, his skin—see a discussion of skin boundaries in Chapter 7). Though he agreed with this idea in principle, he was reluctant to try it, he told me, because he was terrified to take a shower. "Oh!" I responded, "What do you do instead?" "I just hold my breath and take one anyway, as fast as I can," he replied. He was submitting himself to this torture daily. At that point in time I was less interested in why he was scared of the shower than I was in removing this daily terror from his life—giving him some relief. Inquiring further I discovered that he was not afraid of water or washing himself, just the shower. I asked him if he could wash his hair in the kitchen sink and take a sponge bath. Yes, both those would be fine. (Had bathing itself been the issue, a bit more ingenuity would have been required to provide some relief for him within the bounds of good hygiene.) We negotiated that he would cease showering for at least three weeks. After four weeks he reported to me that he had resumed daily showering. He still didn't like it very much, but no longer suffered terror of it. Removing that trigger for a brief period of time was enough to loosen its hold on him.

In the Therapeutic Setting

No trauma therapy can or should take place in the absence of a developed, secure relationship between client and therapist. Of course, it is not possible for a client to fully trust a new therapist; nor is it advisable. But there must be enough basis for trust and some time for each to get used to the other. Some instances of therapeutic failure can be traced to premature introduction of techniques—sometimes during the first meeting. There should be at least one session, preferably a minimum of two or three, before trauma therapy techniques are applied, to allow the client time to get to know and build trust in the therapist. But there is no rule of thumb. Some clients may need years before they are ready to move beyond relationship building to directly addressing traumatic memories.

DEVELOPING AND REACQUAINTING RESOURCES

The more resources the client has, the easier the therapy and the more hopeful the prognosis. When taking a case history it is a good idea to be equally on the lookout for resources as for traumas. It is advisable to evaluate resources and build those that are lacking before embarking on a difficult course of trauma therapy, though, of course, some must be developed along the way. There are five major classes of resources: *functional, physical, psychological, interpersonal,* and *spiritual.*

Functional resources include the practical, like a safe place to live, a reliable car, extra locks, etc. In addition, it may be necessary to provide resources in the form of protective contracts with clients during trauma therapy. This idea stems from Transactional Analysis (Goulding & Goulding, 1997). A trauma client is often confronted with situations that mirror the issues being explored in therapy. It is a mystical, if common, occurrence. The client working on trauma from a car accident has a near miss; the one working on the aftermath of a rape is followed at night, etc. The popular term for this phenomenon is "synchronicity." Safety contracts can be helpful in those circumstances. It may be useful, for example, to make a contract to pay extra attention to safe driving with a client working on PTSD following a car accident, or a contract for extra caution at night with a client who has been assaulted.

Physical strength and agility are examples of physical resources. For some clients, weight training that increases muscle tone will be beneficial. For others, techniques that drill the body in protective movements, such as self-defense training, will be useful adjuncts to trauma therapy. In general, building physical resources will give many clients a greater feeling of confidence.

Daniel had suffered anxiety since surviving a big earthquake. He was hypervigilant, sleeping poorly, and even having trouble bathing. He felt he must be always at the ready for the next quake. As he talked I noticed a dissonance in his posture. He appeared to be leaning back comfortably in his chair, but his feet were placed on the floor in a manner suggestive of preparation to bolt. When I pointed this out to him he agreed that he was not able to relax at any time; he was always preparing to dive under the nearest table or run to the nearest doorway for protection. In addition, right at that moment, his heart rate was elevated and his hands were sweaty. I asked him if he had practiced any of these defensive maneuvers. He had not. I suggested that he do so now, following the impulse in his already defensively positioned feet. He did, bolting toward my office door. He opened it and crouched in the doorway. I encouraged him to repeat that movement several times—chair to doorway to crouch. After three practices I inquired as to his heart rate and hand moisture. Both were normalized. I encouraged Daniel to continue practicing at home and at work, finding the best routes to safety. By the next week his constant vigilance had eased considerably, as he had by then anchored in his body the defensive moves necessary to reach protection during an earthquake.

Psychological resources include (but are not limited to) intelligence, sense of humor, curiosity, creativity (including artistic and musical talents), and almost all defense mechanisms. It is empowering to regard defense mechanisms as the positive coping strategies they once were. Each is a positive resource. The only exceptions are defenses that harm other people. Every defense was, at one time, an (usually successful) attempt to protect the self. The problem with a defense mechanism is not in the mechanism itself, but that it is one-sided, therefore limiting. What is missing with each defense mechanism is the choice of its opposite (Rothschild, 1995b). Three examples:

1. The defense of withdrawal is not a problem in itself—who of us doesn't need to withdraw at times? However, one is at a disadvantage when only able to withdraw and never able to engage with others. On the other hand, the person who is afraid to be alone and must always be in the company of others—who has no capacity to enjoy solitude—is equally handicapped.

2. The person who always expresses anger when stressed is able to defend herself, but sometimes at a cost of alienating others. Though the person who is unable to express anger may avoid alienation, he may be unable to defend himself when necessary. Both strategies are resources.

3. Many would envy an individual who can so dissociate at the dentist that painful work can be done without anesthesia. But, of course, unchecked dissociation of that caliber can cause problems in other areas of daily functioning. What is needed in such an instance is to help the client learn to control his dissociation, maintaining the ability to do it when it is useful (like at the dentist) and being able to stay present when that is safer or more useful (for example, when driving).

The solution to a limiting defense mechanism is not in removing it, but in developing its opposite for both balance and choice. Such a positive view can also help the client who feels ashamed of his defenses.

A client's current social network, including spouse or partner, other family members, and friends, is the core of interpersonal resources. In addition, remembering significant people from the client's past can bring about positive feelings and sensations. Remembered friends, parents, grandparents, teachers, and neighbors can all be powerful resources used to facilitate the therapy. Animals also belong in this category. Pets are often potent sources of resource—especially current pets, but often past pets as well.

Alex's love of rock climbing was cut short when she had a serious fall. She suffered a concussion and broken arm. Four years later she was still plagued by images of her fall, sometimes waking in a cold sweat in the middle of the night. As she told me about it she paled and her breathing quickened. Her husband was not sympathetic. He had never approved of her choice of sport and had been angry when she was injured. That the accident still haunted her was, for him, assurance that she would not go climbing again. As we explored the aftermath of the accident (see Chapter 8 for the rationale behind working with the aftermath of the trauma first), Alex remembered feeling totally abandoned by her husband. His reaction was worse for Alex than her physical injuries. She came home from the hospital in need of care and nurturing, and he was too angry to provide it. He provided for her basic needs but was unable to give her the nurturing support she needed. "How did you survive that?" I asked. "You know," Alex said, "I don't think I would have if it weren't for my Golden Retriever. Solo stayed with me day and night, only leaving my side for short periods of time." I encouraged her to remember Solo's attention now. Where did he lie? How did his fur feel in her hand? Could she remember his warmth? As she remembered her contact with Solo, Alex calmed and cried softly. She felt touched to remember the dog's love for her. Her breathing normalized and color returned to her face.

Spiritual resources include belief in a higher power, following a religious figure, adherence to religious practice, and communing with nature. Sometimes utilizing a client's spiritual resources is difficult for the therapist whose belief system differs. One must come to terms with this countertransferential response, since spiritual resources can be very powerful aids to the healing of traumatic conditions. In addition, some victims of trauma feel betrayed by their beliefs. For those individuals, reclaiming the lost relationship to the spiritual will be a crucial step toward healing.

Sometimes, helping clients with PTSD look at how they have survived their lives and their traumas is a useful adjunct to treatment. Every survivor of trauma has had some role in his or her survival, even if it is by freezing or dissociating. Through such an exercise, many discover how many resources they actually have. The result can be very hopeful. At the least, reminding clients of their resources can prevent despair.

Fifty-year-old Arnold was at the threshold of hospitalization. His downward spiral following a work-related traumatic incident had resulted in a belief that he was totally hopeless and helpless. He feared his ability to cope was so lost that the hospital was his only option. His wife forced him to call me for an appointment, and she had to drive him as his anxiety was too high to come alone. During the intake interview Arnold could only complain about all of the faculties he had lost: He could no longer work, he had lost friends, everyone was giving up on him, he was anxious all the time, he could do nothing for himself. I picked up on that last comment and observed, "I see you are clean shaven. Who shaved you today?" "Why, I did," he replied. "Who dressed you, then?" I asked further. "I dressed myself," he answered a bit suspiciously. I pressed on, "Who fed you your breakfast?" "I didn't eat much," he asserted. "That's okay," I answered, "but what you did eat, who fed you?" "Well I did, of course!" he answered, beginning to get a little irritated with me. By the end of that session Arnold was slightly encouraged. He had so convinced himself of total helplessness, he had forgotten that he was still quite capable of taking care of his own basic needs. Of course this one intervention was no cure, but it was a microstep that enabled Arnold to remain at home.

OASES, ANCHORS, AND THE SAFE PLACE

Oases

Many trauma clients benefit from engaging in activities that give them a break from their trauma. What works will be different for each, but diverting activities have common features. An oasis must be an activity that demands concentration and attention. Watching TV and reading do not usually work well, as it is easy to wander into one's own thoughts. Procedures that have not yet become automatic often do the trick. For example, knitting will work for some, but not for those who have been doing it all their lives—unless, of course, an exceedingly difficult pattern is chosen. For some it will be car repair, for others gardening; many find computer games or solitaire work well. Whatever is chosen, its value as an oasis will be recognized through body awareness (see the next chapter), by the reduction in hyperarousal as well as quieting of internal dialogue.

Anchors

The concept of anchors sprang from neuro-linguistic programming (NLP) (Bandler & Grinder, 1979), but has been adapted for use in several trauma therapies. Basically, an anchor is a concrete, observable resource (as opposed to an internalized resource like self-confidence). It is preferable that an anchor be chosen from the client's life, so that the positive memories in both body and mind can be utilized. Examples include a person (grandmother, a special teacher, a spouse), an animal (favorite pet), a place (home, a site in nature), an object (a tree, a boat, a stone), an activity (swimming, hiking, gardening). A suitable anchor is one that gives the client a feeling (in body and emotion) of relief and well-being.

When working with trauma, it is useful for each client to establish at least one anchor to use as a braking tool anytime the therapy gets rough. Anchors can also be improvised by introducing a previously noted resource.

I noticed that when Cynthia told me about her best friend during the assessment interview her demeanor changed. She had entered the office almost apologetically, fearful and suspicious. She sat hunched, anxious, and pale. When speaking of her friend, though, Cynthia literally expanded; her head straightened and her chest broadened. Color rose to her cheeks and her breathing eased. I drew a star beside my notes about her friend. Later during the interview, Cynthia became quite pale while telling me about the many traumas she had experienced. She reported that her heart was racing. At that point I interrupted and suggested we go back to some of the things she had mentioned previously, "What was your friend's name? I forgot to write it down. Tell me a little more about her." Just naming her friend reduced Cynthia's hyperarousal. While talking about the friend, color returned to Cynthia's face, and she told me her heart rate had decreased.

When she was more relaxed, she was better able to resume naming the traumatic incidents she thought I should know about.

Anchors can also be used to insert a different spin on a traumatic event—not changing the fact of it, but the internal impression.

In a subsequent session further on in Cynthia's therapy, I was again able to make use of her best friend. Cynthia trembled as she related an incident of abuse at the hands of her mother. She had been terrified and too little to defend herself. I asked her, "How would that incident have been different if your best friend had been there?" "Well, that's not possible," Cynthia replied, "I didn't know her then!" I persevered, "Of course, but if you had, and she had been there at the time, how would it have been different?" "Well, she would have stopped my mother completely. My friend is bigger than my mother was, she could have overpowered her!" "If you remember that incident now," I suggested, "and imagine your friend there, how do you feel in your body?" "I feel calmer. (She begins to cry.) I wish she had been there, it was so awful!" The tears were calm and healing. Cynthia was beginning, for the first time, to grieve just how bad it had been.

Inserting an anchor, especially one from the client's current life, cannot—in any way—change reality, but it might give a new impression and help to separate the past trauma from current life.

Applying the anchor is easy. When the hyperarousal gets too high, the therapist just changes the subject. "Let's just stop this for a moment. Tell me about [insert anchor]." The connection can be deepened by giving sensory cues that are associated to the anchor. One of the biggest difficulties of applying anchors is getting used to interrupting the client's "flow." When it is clear how much inserting anchors helps the process, both therapist and client gain greater tolerance for such interruptions. Anchors make it possible to continue addressing difficult memories while periodically lowering the base level of hyperarousal rather than allowing it to build and build. Each time the anchor is used, the hyperarousal lowers. When the client resumes addressing her trauma, it is from a lower level than before the break. In this way, a traumatic memory can be fully addressed without the hyperarousal going out of control.

addressing trauma → hyperarousal → anchor → lowered arousal

Use of the anchor figures prominently in the detailed therapy session at the end of Chapter 6.

The Safe Place

The safe place is a specialized anchor. It was first used in hypnosis for reducing the stress of working with traumatic memories (see, e.g., Napier, 1996). A safe place is a current or remembered site of protection (Jørgensen, 1992). It is preferable for the safe place to be an actual, earthly location that the client has known in life. As such, there will be somatic resonance in the memory of it—sights, smells, sounds, etc., connected to that site will all be recorded as sensory memory traces—which will make it highly accessible and useful to the client. The client can imagine his safe place during times of stress and anxiety, or it can be used as any anchor is used, to reduce hyperarousal during a therapy session.

And When Nothing Works?

A few clients will appear unable to imagine and/or use calming images of anchors and safe places. What may happen with such individuals is that each time they begin to imagine one, it becomes contaminated in some way and feels unsafe. This pitfall can occur when the client believes that the fantasy controls him, rather than that he controls the fantasy. For example, a client with a nurturing grandparent as anchor will suddenly remember a disappointment, or the client will become afraid a safe place in the woods could be invaded. When this happens, the therapist needs to have a frank discussion with the client, first reminding the client that it is his fantasy and he can make it anything he wants, and then explaining that what is required is not the perfect anchor or safe place but one that is "good enough." The fantasy safe place and safe person can be controlled in ways that real life places and people cannot. For example, limit the anchor to the best or ideal memories of the grandparent. Another strategy might be to imagine a barrier (visible or invisible) around the safe place in the woods and/or sentries posted for protection (Bodynamic, 1988–1992). Imagined embellishments that serve to strengthen the calming effect of the anchor or safe place are often useful in these circumstances.

Problems with positive affect tolerance can also limit the usefulness of an anchor or safe place. A small percentage of clients will become anxious when imagining or actually being in positive situations or feeling states. For some PTSD clients it is difficult to differentiate the nervous system responses of positive emotions (happiness, excitement, etc.) from those of anxiety; increased heart rate and respiration can accompany both. Body awareness training (see the next chapter) will help this discrimination, as anxiety is usually accompanied by pallor and decreased temperature in the face and extremities, whereas excitement and happiness are usually accompanied by increased color and temperature.

Another problem with positive affect tolerance occurs when the client fears the good feeling because he anticipates it will not last. Again, body awareness can be useful in helping to recognize that no emotional or somatic state lasts forever. Learning to follow the ebb and flow of somatic sensations may reinforce the idea that emotional states also ebb and flow.

THE IMPORTANCE OF THEORY

One of the ways the therapist can increase the safety of trauma therapy is to be familiar with trauma theory. When the therapist knows what she is doing and why, she is less apt to make mistakes. Theory is more useful than technique, as techniques can fail, but theory rarely lets you down. When one is well versed in the theory of trauma, it is not even necessary to know a lot of techniques, as ideas for interventions will arise from understanding and applying theory to a particular client, at a particular moment, with a particular trauma. Moreover, when a therapist is well versed in theory, it becomes possible to adapt the therapy to the needs of the client rather than requiring the client to adapt to the demands of a particular technique.

Sometimes teaching theory itself to the client will be just what is needed. Teaching theory is especially useful when the client has multiple traumas and is not ready for the use of techniques. Two examples:

Fred had struggled for a while to connect his debilitating physiological reactions to beatings he received as a child. Intellectually he knew that there must be a connection, but he couldn't relate to it. One day he came to therapy very depressed. He was worried because he had become "suicidal"—unusual for him. As we explored his feelings and his body awareness he began to cry, "It's not that I want to die, it's just that I feel so dead inside." A picture formed in my mind. I asked him if he had ever seen a mouse caught by a cat. Having grown up in a rural area, he had seen this many times; he remembered the mouse "playing dead." I asked him to consider the mouse's behavior, which led to a discussion about the autonomic nervous system and the theory of freeze reactions. He was very touched, quickly able to relate to the mouse's talent for surviving by going dead. He remembered doing the same numerous times in response to the beatings. After a few minutes of letting this information sink in, it clicked. Fred realized that he was not suicidal after all, but connecting to his own "mouse." His relief was palpable. That session was a catalyst to his subsequent therapy. Having found a positive explanation for his deadness, he became less afraid to identify other body sensations and their connection to his traumatized past. Previously frightening sensations became friends (like the mouse going dead for survival) rather than enemies.

Scott came to therapy in his early twenties because he lacked self-confidence. A major problem was his inability to pass a driving test; he had failed numerous times. He felt like a failure—all of his friends had passed their tests and begun to drive. His parents were frustrated and could not understand what his problem was. His driving teacher noticed that Scott could drive quite competently at times, but at other times Scott would not even notice a truck right next to him. The teacher was at her wit's end.

On closer probing during our first meeting, Scott described his difficulty as something that sounded akin to a kind of dissociation. He would "space out" and lose track of what he was doing and where he was going. As Scott described this phenomenon to me, he began to dissociate in a similar manner right in the therapy session. He lost track of what he was going to say, became rather pale, and heard my voice from a great distance. I changed the subject, pulling up something positive he had mentioned previously, and he stabilized. He was then able to take up the thread of what he had intended to say.

After taking a case history, which included several incidents of earlier trauma, I proceeded to explain the function of the ANS and the phenomenon of dissociation. Scott was easily able to see his dissociative reaction and speculate its cause. The impact was dramatic. By the next session he had stopped thinking of himself as a bungling and incompetent driver. He realized he had a driving difficulty, not because something was inherently wrong with him, but because he had some past *experiences that were still affecting him adversely. He was able to explain this to his parents and friends, who mostly became more sympathetic. Amazingly, he was able to use the information and the experience of controlling the dissociation during the session to decrease his dissociation while driving. He would distract his thoughts to something positive and then was able to keep his focus on the road. Scott was so successful that soon after he was able to pass his test. Scott, his instructor, parents, and friends were all amazed.*

Moreover, as Scott's perception of his problem changed to one of past traumatic incidents rather than innate ineptitude, his self-perception also changed. He began to see himself as someone having past experiences to deal with rather than being a "bungling fool." That shift gave Scott the courage to take on other tasks, both physical and interpersonal, that he had previously felt were beyond him.

Of course, such dramatic changes are not the norm. But for many, theory is a key that unlocks a wealth of resources.

RESPECTING INDIVIDUAL DIFFERENCES

Therapeutic error can be reduced by never expecting one intervention to work the same for two clients. When a technique does not work, it is advisable for the therapist to look for the failure in the timing, or in the choice of or application of the technique, not in the client. Consider that what this client needs may not yet have been discovered. This perspective will keep the therapist from blaming a client for "resistance." Further, it is a good idea for any therapist working with PTSD to be trained in more than one modality. This will go a long way in assuring that the therapy is tailored to the needs of the client, not vice versa. And, of course, the therapist must be prepared for those times when the best technique is no technique. Sometimes the most effective intervention is just to be with the client talking about mundane things.

TEN FOUNDATIONS FOR SAFE TRAUMA THERAPY

The following list distills the most salient points of safe trauma therapy and serves as a review of this chapter.

1. First and foremost: Establish safety for the client within and outside the therapy.

2. Develop good contact between therapist and client as a prerequisite to addressing traumatic memories or applying any techniques—even if that takes months or years.

3. Client and therapist must be confident in applying the "brake" before they use the "accelerator."

4. Identify and build on the client's internal and external resources.

5. Regard defenses as resources. Never "get rid of" coping strategies/defenses; instead, create more choices.

6. View the trauma system as a "pressure cooker." Always work to reduce—never to increase—the pressure.

7. Adapt the therapy to the client, rather than expecting the client to adapt to the therapy. This requires that the therapist be familiar with several theory and treatment models.

8. Have a broad knowledge of theory—both psychology and physiology of trauma and PTSD. This reduces errors and allows the therapist to create techniques tailored to a particular client's needs.

9. Regard the client with his/her individual differences, and do not judge her for noncompliance or for the failure of an intervention. Never expect one intervention to have the same result with two clients.

10. The therapist must be prepared, at times—or even for a whole course of therapy—to put aside any and all techniques and just talk with the client.

Principles and techniques for increasing client resources, slowing down processes, and applying the brakes follow in the next chapters.

CHAPTER SIX

The Body as Resource

<u>A Toast</u>

The soul may be a mere pretense,
the mind makes very little sense.
So let us value the appeal
of that which we can taste and feel.
—Piet Hein

The potential benefits of being able to use the body as a resource in the treatment of trauma and PTSD, regardless of the treatment model, cannot be overemphasized. In this chapter, non-touch strategies and interventions for increasing somatic resources—making the body an ally—will be presented. Most should find the ideas outlined here to be easily adapted to their own way of working.

BODY AWARENESS

Employing the client's own awareness of the state of his body—his perception of the precise, coexisting sensations that arise from external and internal stimuli—is a most practical tool in the treatment of trauma and PTSD. Consciousness of current sensory stimuli is our primary link to the here and now; it is also a direct link to our emotions. As a therapeutic tool, simple body awareness makes it possible to gauge, slow down, and halt traumatic hyperarousal, and to separate past from present. Moreover, body awareness is a first step toward interpreting somatic memory.

The practice of concentrating on body sensations and body processes is not new. There are many body-oriented therapies that, more and less, use body awareness as the foundation of or adjunct to their methods. The usefulness of cultivating awareness of the state of the body has ancient roots in the Eastern practices of meditation and yoga. The idea of utilizing body awareness as a tool of Western psychotherapy was first introduced by Gestalt therapist Fritz Perls in *Ego, Hunger and Aggression* in 1942. It was then popularized in his 1969 book, *In and Out of the Garbage Pail*. Personal growth exercises based on Perls's awareness principle—following shifts in precise sensory awareness of the internal and external environments—were published two years later in *Awareness: Exploring, Experimenting, Experiencing* by John O. Stevens.

Attention to the body has not commonly been central to the psychotherapeutic treatment of trauma and PTSD. While it is well documented that PTSD goes hand in hand with disturbing bodily sensations and avoidance behaviors (APA, 1994), attention to sensation and movement as a part of the trauma treatment strategy in psychotherapy has not often been proposed.

What Is Body Awareness?

It is difficult to define something as subjective as *body awareness*. The following is a definition that will have to suffice for the purposes of this discussion and future reference in this book:

> Body awareness implies the precise, subjective consciousness of body sensations arising from stimuli that originate both outside of and inside the body.

Body awareness has everything to do with the awareness of cues from the sensory nervous system discussed earlier. Just to refresh your memory, body awareness from exteroceptors originates from stimuli that have their origin outside of the body (touch, taste, smell, sound, sights). Body awareness from interoceptors consists of sensations that originate on the inside of the body (connective tissue, muscles, and viscera). Body awareness is not an emotion, such as "afraid." Emotions are identified by a combination of distinct body sensations:

shallow breathing + elevated heart rate + cold sweat = afraid

Terms that help to identify the various bodily sensations include (but are not limited to):

breathing: location, speed, and depth; position of a body part in space; skin humidity (dry or moist); hot, cold; tense, relaxed; big, small; restless, calm; movement, still; dizzy; shivers, prickles; pressure, pulling; rotation, twist; contraction, expansion; pulse rate, heartbeat; pain, burning; vibration, shaking; weak, strong; sleepy, awake; yawning; tears, crying; light, heavy; soft, hard; tight, loose; crooked, straight; balanced, unsteady; upright, tilted; butterflies; shaky; empty, full

Developing Body Awareness

Many clients already have a good idea of what they sense in their bodies and will be able to communicate this to you. With them, you can go straight to utilizing their body awareness as a resource (see the next section). However, some clients, when asked, "What are you aware of (or sense) in your body right now?" will not know. They may be unable to feel their body sensations at all, or they may feel something but not have the vocabulary to describe the sensations. Others will have so little contact with their bodies that when they are asked that same question, they respond on a totally different topic, "It feels like what I was telling you about my boss last week. . . ."

But do not despair. Most clients can learn to identify and pay greater attention to their sensations. Many will even find the experience quite rewarding. The following exercise illustrates basic body awareness:

- *First, do not move. Notice the position you are sitting in right now*
- *What sensations do you become aware of? Scan your whole body: notice your head, neck, chest, back, stomach, buttocks, legs, feet, arms, hands.*

- *Are you comfortable?—Do not move, yet.*
- *How do you know if you are comfortable or not? Which sensations indicate comfort/discomfort?*
- *Do you have an impulse to change your position?—Do not do it yet, just notice the impulse.*
- *Where does that impulse come from? If you were to change your position, what part of your body would you move first?—Do not do it yet. First follow that impulse back to the discomfort that is driving it: Is your neck tense? Is there somewhere that is beginning to become numb? Are your toes cold?*
- *Now follow the impulse and change position. What changes have occurred in your body? Do you breathe easier? Is a pain or area of tension relieved? Are you more alert?*
- *If you have no impulse to change your position you might just be comfortable. See which bodily cues you get that signal that you are comfortable: Are your shoulders relaxed? Is your breathing deep? Is your body generally warm?*
- *Next, change your position whether or not you are comfortable (again, if you already did it above). Change where or how you are sitting. Move somewhere else: Try a new chair, stand up, or sit on the floor. Take a new position and hold it. Then evaluate again: Are you comfortable or not? Which bodily sensations tell you: tension, relaxation; warmth, cold; ache; numbness; breathing depth and location, etc. This time also notice if you are more alert or awake in this position or in the last one.*
- *Try a third position. Evaluate as above.*
- *Jot a few notes about your experience, keeping in the language of body sensation: tension, temperature, breathing, etc. "When I was sitting in my chair I felt tense in my shoulders and my feet were warm. When I moved to stand on the floor, my feet became cold and my shoulders relaxed. . . ."*

The above exercise can be adapted for clients. It will help many to get the idea of identifying body sensations, though some it will not. Following up the exercise with inquiries about body awareness in subsequent therapy sessions will reinforce and further develop this resource.

For clients who cannot distinguish sensations as they scan their body, specific questions will help: "What is the sensation in your stomach right now?" "What is the temperature of your hands?" "Do you notice where your breath goes?" etc.

With those for whom the whole area of body awareness is just too foreign, frightening, untimely, and/or frustrating, it is often possible to first approach it indirectly. One way to encourage body awareness in such clients is by asking their opinion on room temperature, if the chair cushion is soft or hard, or if they are thirsty and want something to drink. Another strategy for increasing body awareness would be to explore the kinesthetic sense: "Without looking, can you tell how your legs (or hands) are positioned right now?"

Angie was trying to stay away from her abusive husband. Sometimes he would show up where she was staying and she would go with him. It wasn't until later that she realized she had made a mistake. For her it was like she entered an altered state. The fact that she couldn't control her behavior, let alone describe what that state felt like, disturbed her immensely; she felt stupid and ashamed. Body awareness was difficult, generally, for Angie, but despite some anxiety, she was willing to try. I decided not to ask her about her body specifically, as she could quickly become frustrated when she did not produce the "right" answer. Instead I asked, "Can you feel the chair under your buttocks?" That she could feel. I ventured, "What does it feel like?" She was able to describe how the consistency of the cushion felt, as well as that the chair was unsteady since one leg was slightly shorter than the others. "Do you feel more anxious, less anxious, or the same as when you arrived?" She felt slightly less anxious. So far, so good; I could dare a bit more. "You can feel the chair under you now. Do you think that when your husband is around, you would be able to feel the chair?" Her interest increased as she answered the question, "No, I don't think I could. Actually, I don't think I can feel anything when I get around him." For the first time she could describe an aspect of her altered state: the absence of sensation. Already, via this short introduction to her body, it began to make sense to Angie that if she couldn't feel anything in the presence of her husband she would easily acquiesce. This was a microstep on the road to helping her gain control over her life.

In a few instances it will be possible to eliminate some trauma symptoms just by using body awareness. Such an intervention will not necessarily resolve the trauma, but it could go a long way to restoring normal functioning. At that point the client will be in a much more powerful position to decide the direction of his therapy.

Carl began having periodic flashbacks and frequent panic attacks as an adolescent following two bad LSD trips. He had tried medical help to no avail. At 25 he decided to try psychotherapy. After a few sessions Carl became able to identify and describe what it was that initiated the current panic attacks. It was a particular sensation in his gut that he recognized as preceding the onset of a flashback. When he felt that sensation, he feared he was about to have another one and broke into panic. The fact that the actual flashbacks were decreasing in frequency didn't help. That gut sensation scared him and set the panic attacks in motion.

We discussed the alternatives. There were two possible directions the therapy could take: (1) focusing on the here-and-now situation (gut sensation and panic attacks), or (2) delving into the past (the bad LSD trips). Carl did not want to go near memories of those LSD trips, but he was willing to work on his current situation. We further developed his body awareness and explored what the gut sensation felt like, specifically, when it occurred. I asked Carl to become a detective, carefully noting when he got the sensation, what time, under which circumstances, of how long duration, etc. Over the next few weeks he found out that he usually had that sensation around mid-morning on days that he was constipated. On days that he had a morning bowel movement, there was no sensation to contend with, and he would be free of panic. Then the way became clear. The next assignment was for Carl to observe his morning routine and breakfast menu to find out what was different on the non-panic days. This was easy. On mornings that he woke up with at least one and a half hours before he had to leave for work and ate breakfast, he would be fine. On panic mornings he bolted awake with only a half-hour before running out the door, gulping a cup of coffee and skipping breakfast altogether. I proposed that the caffeine kick unmediated by any protein or carbohydrates, plus the drop in blood sugar from skipping breakfast probably added to his vulnerability to panic on those days. Voluntarily, Carl began a strict schedule of early rising and daily breakfast. Within a very short time the panic attacks had disappeared entirely. At that point he decided to take a break from therapy, as his goal had been met. However, his therapy experience was so successful that he was determined to return within the year to address his fears of the flashbacks and the impact of the bad LSD trips themselves.

A caution: There are several situations where teaching body awareness would be contraindicated. Here are two examples (there are certainly others): (1) Some traumas are so damaging to the bodily integrity that any attempt at sensing the body will overly accelerate contact to the trauma(s), causing overwhelming feelings and risking decompensation; (2) there are clients who will feel pressured to sense their body "correctly" and so develop a kind of performance anxiety. With such clients, the task of developing body awareness must be laid aside in favor of work with the basics outlined in the previous chapter—developing safety, establishing the therapeutic relationship, building internal and external resources, finding oases. Later, when such clients are feeling calmer, delving into the daunting territory of body sensation usually becomes more manageable.

MAKING FRIENDS WITH SENSATIONS

As can be seen from the above case example, clients with PTSD, particularly those with anxiety and panic attacks, often come to identify their current body sensations as dangerous when they remind them of previous trauma. When it is not possible to distinguish safe sensations from dangerous ones, all sensations may become perceived as dangerous. Through well-timed and paced body awareness training, a client can be reintroduced to the friendly function of sensations.

Sensations are a gauge. They tell us when we are tired, alert, hungry, full, thirsty, sated, cold, warm, comfortable, uncomfortable, happy, sad, etc. With clients who are scared to feel their sensations, or those who wish they had none, imagining the consequences of being unable to feel pain or the sensations that indicate fear can be illuminating. *How would you know the pot was too hot to touch? You could get burned and not know it. How would you know where the limits of exercise were? Injuries would be common. How would you know not to walk on a deserted street alone or not to approach a dog on the street if you could not feel fear?* It does not take long to realize that life would be very dangerous if these sensations and emotions could not be perceived.

With graduated body awareness training clients become familiar with their body sensations. Usually they discover that the better acquainted they are with them, the less scary they become.

Body Awareness as the Basis of Identifying Emotions

You may remember from the discussion in Chapter 3 of Damasio's theory of somatic markers that each emotion has a discrete set of body sensations associated with it, though individual body sensations may be shared by several emotions. With clients who are unable to identify and name their emotions (the clinical term is *alexithymic*), establishing body awareness is invaluable.

One strategy for helping clients to identify emotions involves taking advantage of situations in which the therapist observes an expression of emotion in the client: facial expression, posture, tone of voice. This is a good time to interrupt the current discussion or procedure and ask the client, "What are you aware of in your body right now?" or, more specifically, "Did you notice your breathing just change (or heat rise in your face, or how hard it was to swallow just then)?" Gradual association of body states may accumulate until the client experiences several at one time. At that point the client can be asked if he has experienced those sensations together earlier in his life, and if so, what emotion he was feeling then. Another possibility is to externalize the experience by asking the client what someone else would be feeling if that person had those same body sensations.

THE BODY AS ANCHOR

Awareness of current body sensations can anchor one in the present, here and now, facilitating separation of past from present. One is less likely to stay lost or stuck in the past while aware of body sensations. This is very important when working with trauma and PTSD, since the pull into the memories of the past can be great and decompensation severe. Sensing the body is a current-time activity. One can remember a sensation, but one feels the remembered sensation *now*. Of course, some clients will require an added reminder of that when the sensations trigger a flashback.

Body Awareness as Anchor vs. Accelerator

This next brief installment, Charlie and the Dog, Part III (continued from pp. 45–46), illustrates the use of body awareness as an anchor.

Helping Charlie to focus on his body awareness was critical to calming and thawing his frozen state. I repeatedly directed his attention to his body, "What is happening in your body right now? And what else are you aware of?" His legs were stiff, his breathing restricted, his mouth was dry, and his heart was racing. Luckily, Charlie had a well-developed sense of his body and we used it to great advantage. I kept leading him back to the same areas to evaluate nuances of change in legs, breath, heart, and mouth. The more he scanned his body, the calmer he felt. Round after round, his legs loosened, his breathing and heart rate relaxed; only the dryness in his mouth persisted without relief.

When anchoring is the goal, body awareness inquiry must be fairly quick paced—not speeding, but not allowing the client to focus on any one sensation for very long. The question must also be phrased in the present tense. The aim is to keep the client in the here and now. This type of quick body awareness query is used to "pft" or reduce some of the pressure. The opposite, going slowly, staying with one sensation a long time, risks stirring up more memories. (*That would have been contraindicated for Charlie, as he was not ready to handle more at that time—the pressure cooker was already at maximum pressure.*)

Contrary to expectation, clients usually become less, rather than more, anxious when encouraged to notice and describe their body sensations under this quick scan method. Once they become adept at it, many clients report that during trauma therapy it is a relief for them to shift focus to current sensations. Body awareness can become a secure link to the present.

Body awareness can also be used to reinforce the anchors and safe places as discussed above. The greater the degree of positive body sensations associated to them, the greater calming effect they will have.

THE BODY AS GAUGE

Monitoring the client's body sensations, particularly those that identify the state of the autonomic nervous system (ANS) (see Figure 3.1, p. 38), provides a dependable guide to the pacing of the therapy.

The ability to recognize indications of hyperarousal, ANS overactivation, is an easily acquired skill. But like any skill it takes practice. By noticing what is happening in the client, the therapist secures a valuable, objective gauge for reading the client's arousal state. It can also be useful to teach the client to recognize signs of ANS activation in himself—to gain a greater sense of body awareness and of self-knowledge and control.

The ANS is not the only usable gauge in trauma therapy. It can be useful to note other types of body awareness: tightness, stomach upset, changes in vision or hearing, etc. Sometimes sticking with one sensation, tracking changes in it as the therapy progresses, will be useful (see the detailed session at the end of this chapter).

Limitations

Therapist observation combined with client sensory feedback on the state of the ANS is one of the most powerful tools available to the trauma therapist for pacing the therapy. But there are certain limitations to those observations.

Observing skin tone is a major tool for evaluating the state of the ANS, as the skin—particularly of the face—is usually quite available to the eye of the therapist. Of course, this is easier with light-toned skin; however, dark skin also flushes and pales. It is just a matter of attuning the eye to recognize it. A dark skin doesn't blush in the same way a light skin does. With the increase of blood flow to the skin, it darkens. Likewise, it doesn't blanch white, but when it loses the red pigment caused by blood flow, it becomes more gray than brown.

The visually handicapped therapist is, of course, limited in the task of observing ANS arousal. However, some of those limitations can be converted into advantages. The client must supply the information that the therapist cannot observe firsthand, giving him practice in noticing and reporting sensations. A similar problem arises with clients whose hyperarousal is clearly worsened by eye contact. With these clients, turning about or changing the direction of the therapist's gaze for a time can be very helpful. When that happens, take advantage of the situation: "It is just fine for me not to look at you. However, since I can't see you, I'll need a little help. Tell me, what is the temperature in your face right now?" (Elevated temperature goes hand-in-hand with more flush; cold skin with pale.) "Where is your breath going mostly—is your chest moving up and down or your stomach moving out and back?" etc. Clients in that situation are usually happy to help—even when their body awareness skills appear to be minimal under other circumstances.

Gauging and Pacing Hyperarousal

Gauging the ANS through observation and the client's body awareness can increase reliability of the popular SUDS scale (Subjective Units of Disturbance Scale) (Wolpe, 1969). As its title indicates, this is a subjective measure. The client gives his opinion of his emotional state on a 1–10 scale, 1 = totally calm, 10 = the most disturbed possible. By observing the ANS, both visually and with client feedback on sensory awareness, the therapist secures an additional measure. It is not uncommon, for example, for clients to give a low SUDS rating while hearts race or hands are clammy (signs of high ANS arousal), which might indicate underlying anxiety that is being dissociated in some way. Using both SUDS and ANS observation gives the therapist important information when there is agreement and when there is disagreement.

Once you learn the indicators, good pacing of the therapy is possible only when those tools are applied. The following is an example of what can go wrong.

Grette was assaulted as a small child. A mass of emotional problems ensued as she grew up. She came to therapy in her early thirties quite decompensated and terrified to confront memories of the assault. After many, many sessions of helping her to stabilize, develop a therapeutic relationship, etc., she came to therapy one day with newfound courage to tell me about the incident. I listened to her, both moved and transfixed. I was pleased that she felt ready to delve into her trauma and I was curious about what she would reveal. In my interest, I forgot one of my own rules of thumb: Sometimes it is better to contain my curiosity. I also neglected to monitor her ANS reactions and to periodically help her to apply the brakes. Despite my peripheral awareness of her gradually paling and increasingly immobile face, I let her talk on. By the end of the session, her once animated features were frozen into a mask. She said that she was okay, if feeling a little "weird." After she left the session, it didn't take long for the anxiety to hit. The rest of the week was filled with panicked phone calls.

All that was needed to make Grette's discourse containable was monitoring of her growing hyperarousal and increasing facial tension. Periodic pauses, diverting to an anchor, safe place, or other resource, before hyperarousal got too high would have changed the therapeutic result completely. It would have been easy to take breaks—and put on the brakes. And even if she had not been able to finish her whole story, she would have had a much easier week.

Interrupting a client in such a fashion prevents the level of arousal from climbing to the point of dissociation or freezing or becoming overwhelming. Periodic breaks, braking, and resource building lowers the arousal level. Continued intervention of this type throughout a therapy session makes it possible for the client to work with terrifying memories at a greater level of comfort.

When observing the client and asking about body awareness, it is fairly simple to evaluate the state of the ANS. The following outlines a scale of arousal to hyperarousal:

- *Relaxed system*—primarily moderate activation of parasympathetic nervous system (PNS). Breathing is easy and deep, heart rate is slow, skin tone is normal.
- *Slight arousal*—signs of low to moderate PNS activation combined with low-level sympathetic nervous system (SNS) activation. Breathing or heart rate may quicken while skin color remains normal; skin may pale and moisten slightly without increases in respiration and pulse, etc.
- *Moderate hyperarousal*—primarily signs of increased SNS arousal: rapid heart beat, rapid respiration, becoming pale, etc.
- *Severe hyperarousal*—primarily signs of very high SNS arousal: accelerated heart beat, accelerated respiration, pale skin tone, cold sweating, etc.
- *Endangering hyperarousal*—signs of very high activation of both

SNS and PNS, for example: pale (or reduced color) skin (SNS) with slow heart rate (PNS); widely dilated pupils (SNS) with flushed color (PNS); slow heart rate (PNS) with rapid breathing (SNS); very slow respiration (PNS) with fast heart rate (SNS), etc.

A relaxed system indicates the client is calm and that the therapy is progressing at a comfortable rate. Slight arousal indicates excitement and/or containable discomfort. A primarily relaxed or slightly aroused PNS system might include emotions of sadness, anger, or grief. Most clients are stable enough to tolerate slight arousal. Moderate arousal may mean the client is having trouble dealing with what is going on and may be quite anxious; it may be time to apply the brakes. Severe arousal is a sign that it is time to hit the brakes with any client.

Endangering arousal is a sign that the client is in a highly traumatized state; the process is speeding out of control. He is likely experiencing some type of flashback (in images, body sensations, emotions, or a combination), which could lead to panic, breakdown, or tonic immobility. High states of arousal might also include emotions of rage, terror, or desperation. At this point one must apply the brakes, either through body awareness and/or strategies that are addressed in the next chapter. Before sending the client home or continuing with the exploration or working through of trauma memories, the therapist must help him stabilize. Stabilization is indicated by either low sympathetic activation or primarily parasympathetic activation. One purpose of learning to observe the bodily signs of ANS arousal is to become competent in avoiding this highly traumatized (and possibly retraumatizing) state, slowing down the therapy before that state is reached.

During a therapy session, while working with a trauma, Bob became noticeably flushed in his face and upper chest (he was wearing a v-neck shirt). He reported feeling heat in the front of his face and trunk, and an elevated heart rate. I could also see that his breathing was very quick and shallow—signs of high activation in both SNS and PNS. The client was experiencing a high degree of discomfort, and I could see it. We hit the brakes by changing the topic to one that reminded him of his strengths and resources. Once he was calmer (his color, breathing, and heart rate mostly normalized), he returned to the difficult topic. It took a few sessions, shuttling back and forth between the traumatic material and the brakes, but even-tually both Bob and I knew we had reached a resolution. Finally, while again addressing the traumatic material, his heart rate, color, and temperature remained in PNS ranges, and his breathing deepened and slowed—all signs of normal PNS activation. He could feel and I could see that his SUDS had dropped to 0.

The purpose of hitting the brakes and dropping the level of arousal is not just to give a pause and a sense of safety. It also, as with the above example, enables the therapy to proceed at a reduced level of arousal. Without hitting the brakes, arousal will just build and build (see Figure 6.1).

Figure 6.1. Addressing the trauma in therapy.

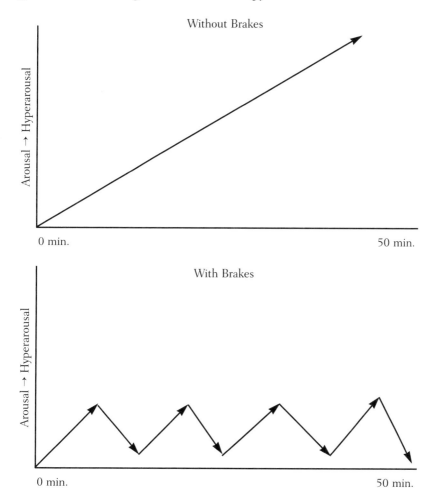

Pacing the Trauma Narrative

In retelling the circumstances of a traumatic event, the greater the amount of detail the client uses, the greater the risk of hyperarousal. ANS monitoring with the option of braking will go a long way toward making this process tolerable and digestible for the client. Dividing a narrative into three stages will also help control the process: (1) name the trauma, (2) outline the trauma by designating titles to the main incidents, (3) fill in the details of each incident, one at a time.

First have the client just name the trauma (e.g.,*"I was injured during a terrorist bombing"*). Observe and ask for feedback on the client's body state. If there is hyperarousal already, the client is not in a psychophysical condition to narrate any more of the story. Stabilization, muscle toning, building trust and safety should be the priority.

If, however, the client can name the incident without significant arousal or dissociation, or if emotion discharges in a managable catharsis and the arousal drops, the next step is to outline the main topics of the trauma—again, without details:

> *"There was an explosion."*
> *"I was hit by shrapnel and thrown against the ground."*
> *"Paramedics thought I was dead and passed me by."*
> *"I was able to call for help and was then attended to."*
> *"At the hospital my mother got hysterical and called me stupid for being in that area of town."*

Sometimes it will be difficult for a client to keep to the titles; instead she will digress into details. It may be necessary for the therapist to interrupt, holding the client within the parameters of the task and containing potential hyperarousal. Even when the client wants to tell the whole story in detail at once, it may not be a good idea. If a client insists, sometimes it will be best to let her go ahead, sometimes not. A better idea may be to explain the rationale of pacing to the client and encourage her to monitor her own responses. Monitoring the ANS and other somatic signs will be a good gauge. It is best to not go any faster than the client's ANS can handle. It is also preferable to set a pace that facilitates the client's ability to make sense out of her responses and the events that caused them.

Finally, when the client is ready—which could be immediately or only after many years—the client narrates each incident in detail while both she and the therapist monitor her level of hyperarousal:

> *"There was an explosion. It was deafening. I felt it before I heard it. I didn't have time to be scared because everything happened so fast. Every-one was screaming—I couldn't hear them because of the blast, but I could see mouths opened in anguish. I tried to move, but I couldn't. I nearly fainted . . ."*

During this step, it will be important for the therapist to periodically interrupt the client and check the level of ANS arousal. If an anchor has been estab-lished, it can be used during breaks to calm any hyperarousal, which makes continuing with the narrative easier for the client. Clients usually report that this strategy gives them a sense of control over their memories that was not possible before.

THE BODY AS BRAKE

The following case, reprinted from an earlier article (Rothschild, 1993), illus-trates how simple body awareness can be used to reduce hyperarousal and halt persistent panic attacks.

A young woman was referred to me for therapy because of panic attacks and ago-raphobia. Initially our work involved focusing on building her body awareness, increasing her boundaries, and establishing a network of friends. The body awareness work involved structured increase of tolerance for her body sensations, which she was quite frightened of. We would discuss an issue and keep return-ing to her sensations to notice how they changed from topic to topic. If she became anxious, we would stay with the sensations until they subsided. After a short time she was able to move into her own apartment and begin a job that was close to her home.

After five months she came to therapy and announced that the previous week at work she had the worst panic attack of her life. She proceeded to describe in precise bodily detail the course of the attack: where the anxiety began, what happened in her breathing, heart rate, muscles, temperature. She ended the report, "I became very warm all over, and then it ended"—it had lasted only one or two minutes. She was tremendously proud of herself. It was the first time in her long history of such attacks that she was able to follow a course of panic to its conclusion. She never knew that it was possible or that a panic attack was actually so short. To my knowledge, although she experienced occasional anxiety, she never had a panic attack again.

THE BODY AS DIARY: MAKING SENSE OF SENSATIONS

Through its sensory storage and messaging system, the body holds many keys to a wealth of resources for identifying, accessing, and resolving traumatic experiences.

Identifying traumatic triggers is one of the great challenges of trauma therapy. Stimuli from the environment can inadvertently set off a traumatic reaction in a client. Often the client is left with the reaction but has no idea what caused it. Tracing the reaction back to the source, the trigger, can be an important task. To that end, body awareness can be a useful assistant. The following protocol is useful for identifying triggers:

- Notice what you feel in your body right now. Be as precise as possible, particularly with regard to disturbances in breathing, heart rate, and temperature.
- Think back and identify when you were last feeling calm—that is point A.
- Identify, approximately, when you began to feel disturbed—that is point B.
- Shuttle back and forth between points A and B, taking note of all aspects of your environment: people, conversation, objects, behaviors. Recall, also, what you were thinking about each step of the way. Notice your body awareness as you focus on each aspect.

- For each element, ask yourself, "Is this what upset/scared/disturbed me?" and notice your bodily and emotional response.
- You will likely identify the triggering element by an increase now in disturbing body sensations and/or an increase in emotion.

This protocol doesn't work for everyone, but it is very useful for many of my clients, particularly those with panic and anxiety attacks.

Sarah used this procedure after she saw a film that left her in a highly distressed state. Her heart raced for the duration of the evening after seeing the film, much to her confusion. It was no mystery that the disturbance arose in the course of the movie (she had been quite calm beforehand), but she couldn't grasp just what it was that had upset her, or why. As she had learned in therapy, before going to bed (sleep would have been difficult in her hyperaroused state anyway), she sat alone and retold herself, aloud, the story of the film. It was toward the end of the retelling that her tears gushed forth and she began to tremble. The source of her upset was a bit of a surprise, but made sense—a neglected corner of her history that had been illuminated by the light of the film. She suspected she had hit the right spot, for when she stopped crying her pulse had again returned to normal and remained so. She made a note of the incident to take up in therapy later that week. After a nurturing cup of chamomile tea, she had a good night's sleep.

Through simple body awareness and shuttling between point A (before the film) and point B (after the film), Sarah identified the source of her upset. It was the reminder of an unresolved issue from earlier in her life. Identification of the trigger halted the anxiety, and she was able to contain the issue until her therapy session later that week.

Sensations can also be used to make sense of somatic memory. This is often facilitated by slow body awareness inquiry. The client stays with any one sensation a minute or more to see what emerges. An example:

Sixty-year-old Donna was still mourning the death, five years earlier, of her husband of 35 years. It had been a shocking blow. He had a heart attack while a passenger in the car she was driving. She had driven like a maniac in an attempt to get him to an emergency room before he died. Of course we spent a lot of time processing the incident and her grief. She also suffered a persistent right hip problem, which caused chronic pain. The condition had emerged about one year after her husband's death. Each in a series of orthopedists, chiropractors, and acupuncturists had helped a little, but the pain persisted. She decided she wanted to see if I could help with that, too. I had her focus on the hip, describing the sensations and being as specific as she could about the pain—its type, location, if it was steady or throbbing, etc. Inspired by Levine's SIBAM model (discussed in Chapter 4), I investigated other aspects of her consciousness. While she stayed focused on the hip pain, I asked about other sensations in her body. It seemed that the more she focused on the pain, the faster her heart beat. I also asked her to notice what emotions she was feeling. She was scared. I had her just stay with those sensations a few minutes: pain, heart rate, fear. As she persisted her right foot dug deeper and deeper into my carpet. It wasn't long before she took a huge breath and began to sob, "I drove as fast as I could. I floored the accelerator. It was an old car and I just couldn't get it to go faster!" It became very clear that a significant part of her hip problem was this memory of bearing down on the gas pedal. This work didn't cure her physical problem completely, as she had been holding that leg tension for four years. But the pain eased and medical treatment became more effective. The session also facilitated her mourning process. She was able to release some of the guilt she had harbored for not making it to the hospital soon enough.

SOMATIC MEMORY AS RESOURCE

The term *somatic memory* is usually associated with the memory of frightening traumatic events. But the body also remembers positive feelings. Awareness of body sensations can be a superhighway to the past, a tool for helping the client connect not only with forgotten traumatic memories but also with forgotten resources.

Remembering how safe and secure it felt to sit in grandma's kitchen—with an emphasis on the comfortable body sensations—may be even more important to current functioning than remembering a frightening incident. Sometimes a positive somatic memory can help an individual resolve a current difficulty without having to confront the terrifying traumatic memory that is triggering it.

Then, eventually, if the client decides to work with the traumatic incident, the successful use of the positive memory can be used to help ease the terror.

Tom had to ask his boss for a raise. He couldn't afford to continue his job at the same rate of pay. And he had put off the confrontation too long as it was. Tom's father had been rather tyrannical and had beaten Tom severely when he had shown any signs of aggression. The idea of having to assert himself at work left Tom weak with fear. We decided, at this particular juncture in his therapy, that it would be more useful to build up his resources than to work on his father issues.

I asked Tom to remember if there was any time when he had been able to safely and successfully assert himself. His biggest triumph in this arena had been five years earlier, when, gathering his courage, he had asked a woman he was attracted to out on a first date. She later became his wife, and he was still very much in love with her. I helped him recall, in both body and mind, how afraid he had been before he asked her out, and how victorious and proud he felt afterward. He made some slight movements with his feet as he recalled leaving her door after their first date. I drew his attention to the movement. Was he aware of it? No, he had not been, but when I mentioned it he was. I encouraged him to repeat the movement and then to slightly exaggerate it. He recognized it immediately. He had virtually danced down the stairs of her apartment building after their first date, and his feet were, subtly, remembering their celebration. How did he feel as his feet danced? Great! Excited, confident, relaxed.

Next came the challenge. I suggested he imagine approaching his boss for the raise while dancing with his feet. He still felt anxious but less so, and he was able to feel a little excited at the idea of a challenge. Now, of course, it would not be prudent for Tom to "dance his way" into his boss's office. So we worked on refining the dance movement down into very subtle small turns of toe and heel that he could, without drawing attention, make while he was talking with his boss, whether sitting or standing.

When he eventually approached his boss the next week, he did get his raise— not as much as he asked for, but acceptable. He was also very proud of himself. He had been scared, but making the subtle dance movements with his feet had reinforced his memory of successful assertion as well as the love and support of his wife, and that had helped him persevere.

FACILITATING TRAUMA THERAPY USING
THE BODY AS RESOURCE

The following case illustrates the application of body awareness, braking, and an anchor to reduce the distress of addressing a traumatic memory. Therapists will be able to recognize where their own disciplines would fit well: extending exposure, using bilateral stimulation, suggesting viewing the memory from a distance, etc. Explanatory comments regarding the therapist's intention and/or theory are identified by italic print in parentheses.

> *(Gail is a forty-something mother of two. She had been wanting for some time to face dealing with a car accident that happened when she was 18. She is just now feeling prepared to confront it. G = Gail, T = Therapist.)*
>
> T: Are you okay with how we are sitting? (I am sitting in a chair, while G had chosen a spot on the floor.)
>
> *(Establishing safety by attending to boundaries, position, and distance.)*
>
> G: No. You're too far away and we're uneven in height.
>
> T: How do you want to change that? (G comes closer and moves from the floor to a chair.)
>
> *(Giving the client control where possible.)*
>
> G: This distance feels good.
>
> T: How do you know it feels good?
>
> *(Connecting body awareness to cognitive evaluation.)*
>
> G: Because I don't feel myself leaning forward or leaning back.
>
> T: Okay. What do you want from this session?
>
> *(Client control: working on what G wants to work on.)*
>
> G: To work with that car accident that happened when I was a teenager. It's still really affecting me.
>
> T: How does that feel in your body when you say that? Sounds like you're making a commitment.
>
> G: Scary.
>
> T: What do you feel in your body that tells you you're scared?
>
> *(Connecting body awareness to emotions.)*
>
> G: My hands feel clammy and sweaty, and I just feel jittery in here

(points to chest). I think, "do I really want to do this?" And I
also feel jittery across my shoulders.

T: Do you really want to do this?

G: YEAH!! (Smiles)

T: How do you feel the part that does? That comes across differently when you smile and say, "YEAH!"

(*Reinforcing the part that is up to the challenge of facing the trauma.*)

G: That accident affected me in lots of ways and I don't want that
effect in my life.

T: How does that feel in your body when you say that? Does the
jitteriness feel the same?

G: No, it's less.

T: So you can be in touch with the part of you that does want to
go ahead and work through this?

G: Yes.

T: Can you also feel the part that doesn't?

(*Acknowledging and containing both realities for G: Part of her wants
to face and work through the trauma; part of her doesn't. That's true
for almost everyone with almost any trauma. Trauma work is rewarding, but not particularly fun.*)

G: I can feel my heart beat faster. I feel scared. I'm thinking, I
don't know what this means. I don't know what this means.

T: Okay. And do you know why you want to work with this now?
Why you think it's important to address it?

(*Engaging the part of G that wants to confront the accident. That
part will be a resourceful ally when the process gets more difficult.*)

G: I keep getting scared people will hurt themselves. I know I do
that when my kids are being adventurous. I get afraid they won't
know their limits and will get hurt. That's exactly what happened
in the car accident. I didn't respect a limit. I now know it's connected with that. I can do something about that! I realize that
accident has had a lot of power in my life, and now I feel I can
deal with it.

T: What you said a minute ago was, "I can do something about
that!"

G: That's what it feels like, I can do something about this. It feels within my power to do something about it.

T: Say that sentence, "I can do something about that!" and see what it feels like in your body.

(Supporting G's confidence that she is ready to deal with this now by connecting to her body sense.)

G: It feels like I have the power to do something about it.

T: How do you sense that power in your body?

G: I feel it in here (points to chest).

T: The same spot as the jitteriness?

G: Yes.

T: How does that feel there?

G: It feels good; it really feels really good that I have the power to do something.

T: And you feel that power here (I point to my chest), just to the left?

G: Yes.

T: Okay. Let's go on then. If we get into a place in working with this that you feel pretty uncomfortable: anxious, stiff (possible freezing), or whatever, how could we take a vacation, a break, from that? Is there any topic I could bring you into that is a source of strength or good feelings for you?

(Establishing an anchor for when the trauma work becomes too distressing.)

G: Nature, trees, a walk in the woods.

T: Is there a particular path you like to walk on?

G: With a clear stream and lots of rocks, trees . . .

T: Are you remembering a particular place?

G: Yes. There is one place that's my favorite.

T: How do you feel in your body when you speak about it?

(Bringing in as many body senses as possible when connecting and reconnecting with an anchor: sight, hearing, touch, smell, taste, movement, posture.)

G: I feel very nice (laughs). I feel myself smiling.

T: I think we can go forward a little now. Do you think so too?

(Again, giving G the control, even while I am steering.)

G: Yes.

T: Okay. First, I would like to hear a very brief outline of the accident—*not* the details.

(Holding her to the edge of connection with the trauma at this point, not allowing G to fall too deeply into the memory. Not going deeper than G has resources—cognitive, physical, and emotional—to handle.)

G: I was in my late teens. I was driving. The car hit a soft shoulder. I lost control and it flipped about three times. I was stuck in the car until somebody got me out.

T: What happens in your body when you tell me the outline?

G: My heart is beating a lot faster. My palms are sweaty again. I feel something here (points to head).

(Even when keeping to an outline she experiences a lot of arousal in the ANS.)

T: Can you still see me?

G: Yes . . . but you're not as clear as you were.

T: Something happened with your eyes, I can see it.

(I saw G's eyes lose their focus.)

G: I feel like I'm further away from you.

T: Is there any physical sensation with feeling further away?

G: No. If anything it's more like a sense of tunnel-y-ness.

T: With your eyes? Like retreating in a tunnel?

G: Yes.

(G may be at the edge of dissociating and/or freezing. Time to divert to the anchor.)

T: Where was that place you like to walk?

G: (Names and describes the location of a river.)

T: Are there particular kinds of rocks or trees there that you like?

G: The rocks are granite, and they are really big. I like to step across the rocks and sit on the ones in the middle of the river; the water moves all around me.

T: How are you feeling in your body right now?

G: Really different. I've got sort of tingly feelings in my arms.

T: A positive kind of tingly?

G: Yes. And a lot cooler.

T: How's our distance right now?

(Checking to see if G has associated again.)

G: I'm closer again, and you're clearer. And I can feel the smile on my face.

T: Okay. Good. So, it works?

(Reassuring both G and myself that the anchor technique is effective.)

G: Yeah. (laughs)

T: Is it okay we go back a little bit to the accident?

(Steering the process, I take G back to the trauma after the break.)

G: Yes.

T: What happened after the accident? You said you were stuck. You got out sometime, you know that?

(It is my preference to explore the events after a traumatic event first. Often the events after are as or more traumatizing than the traumatic event itself. And it is in the wake of the traumatic event that decisions and changes in the belief system are often made. See Chapter 8 for a more detailed discussion of this strategy.)

G: Yes, I was conscious the whole time, but I can't remember who got me out. Then we rode in an ambulance or a police car. My friend kept asking the same 4 questions, over and over again. I could tell that was really driving the policeman crazy (laughs). I sort of went into shock at that time. I started to feel nauseous and all that. The policeman was worried I had internal injuries, but he kept being distracted by my friend.

T: Was your friend in the car? *(A new piece of information emerges.)*

G: Yeah, but I was driving. I was officially a learner, I was just about to take my test.

T: I stick on your saying, "but I was driving." Did you stick on that too?

(A suspicion worth checking out. There are often decisions, judgments, or beliefs connected to feelings of responsibility.)

G: Yes. It's really relevant because we'd made a contract to switch at (names a junction before the accident). But I had been doing so well and was enjoying it so much that we decided I'd drive further. It was after that we had the accident.

T: How are you feeling in your body right now?

G: Weird in my stomach, something about making that decision for me to drive on, if we hadn't . . .

T: What does that mean to you, that you two had an agreement and then decided to go beyond the agreement, and that it was in the part where . . .

G: . . . beyond the limit we'd set . . .

T: . . . "beyond the limit" you'd set that you had the accident?

(*Understanding the* meaning *of a traumatic event is often crucial to integrating that event into the continuum of one's life.*)

G: When I say that I can feel anger at myself for not sticking to a limit I set.

T: What do you sense in your body?

G: Not much. It's not a body anger. More like a criticism, "Why do I do that?"

T: I want to do a little reality check with you: Do you think that had anything to do with the accident?

(*Reality testing can be very useful, challenging a client's view, conclusion, judgment.*)

G: Totally!

T: Why?

G: Because just going onto the shoulder shouldn't have made us flip. I didn't know how to control a car in a skid. But my friend had done a lot of driving and could have controlled a skid. I don't believe my friend would have driven off the edge in the first place—there was no reason to. I'd been distracted and lost my concentration.

T: How are you feeling in your body right now?

G: Okay.

T: How's our distance?

G: Our distance is fine. And you're clear. I think this is interesting.

T: It sounds like you think that you were distracted, but that you went over the shoulder and into a skid because you'd gone over your limit. Is it possible that could have happened also in the stretch before you'd come to the agreed limit?

G: Oh. It could have happened then, too. But the area where the accident happened was much less safe. I hadn't said that. On the other side of the road where we flipped over there was a long drop down to a raging river. In the stretch I'd agreed to drive, there were no drop-offs.

T: And how are you feeling in your body right now?

G: A bit more nauseous. It turned out okay, but what might have happened!?

(This is something to come back to. Some of G's trauma response might come from imagining contingencies. But first, I'm concerned about the nausea.)

T: And our distance?

G: I'm a bit further back, but not as far as I was. You kind of go dark. Your face stays white, but the rest of you goes dark.

(Possible edge of dissociating, again. Time to go back to the anchor.)

T: Let's talk about a *different* river.

G: (Laughs)

T: What was the name of that one you like?

G: (Names it again and we discuss its difficult pronunciation).

T: What color are the rocks?

G: White with speckles of gray and lots of moss on them.

T: Are there also trees?

G: Yes. Oak. Oak forest. I've probably spent more time there with the leaves off the trees than on. A lot of winter walks.

T: What time of day do you like to walk?

G: Anytime I can.

T: In light? In dark?

G: Only in light.

T: Are there any smells?

G: I find it really hard to imagine smells.

T: How do you feel right now?

G: More here, but still a little distant. I want to tell you what I can

do. I can't do smells, but I can tell you what I feel. I can feel
the moistness, the humidity.

T: Where do you feel that humidity?

G: On the skin of my arms and face, in my hands.

T: How's our distance?

G: Much better.

(*G told me at a later date just how significant it had been to be able
to connect with the senses that were available, not focus on the ones
that weren't. Everyone varies in which senses are more prominent—
some more visual, some more tactile, some more auditory, etc.*)

T: Are you ready to go back a little bit?

G: Yes.

T: I wanted to ask you, you said this stretch you were driving on
was much more dangerous than the stretch you had been driving on before. Did you and your friend know that when you
two made the decision that you would continue to drive?

G: Yes.

T: Who's responsible for the decision?

(*Assigning sensible responsibility is often crucial to working through
a trauma.*)

G: I guess it was pretty mutual. We discussed it.

T: How do you feel in your body right now?

G: Fine.

T: Does that mean anything to you, that the decision was mutual?

(*I wanted G to connect her new statement with her previous judgment.*)

G: Not really. I'm thinking maybe it should after what I said earlier, but it . . .

T: About what that you said earlier?

G: About that I can be angry with myself for going over my limits.

T: I was thinking the same thing. Do you know why I would ask
you about that?

(*I will often ask a client if he knows why I asked a question. I'm not
wanting to start a guessing game, and will answer my question if the
client is not able to. However, the question is often useful in helping
the client's cognitive process.*)

G: Because it wasn't only my responsibility. It was *our* responsibility. It seemed a reasonable decision. And, in fact, I don't know if that stretch actually was more dangerous than the other stretch I drove. They're dangerous in different ways. There's a lot less traffic on that stretch of road. There was a lot of traffic on the road before the junction. Differently dangerous. Oh! That feels nice.

(*A dramatic change in G's making sense of the accident.*)

T: How does that "nice" feel, in your body?

G: More relaxed. It was an understandable decision.

(*The change in judgment seems congruent, as G's body sense has also changed.*)

T: It wasn't far-out?

G: It wasn't far-out.

T: How are you feeling about what we've done so far?

G: It's really interesting. It's less of a big deal. I realize I've been blaming myself that if I hadn't been driving it wouldn't have happened. That's why I haven't been trusting my driving now. That's important.

T: I think, this is a good stopping point.

G: Yes, that feels right for me as well.

T: How's our distance?

G: We're both here.

T: How's your heart rate?

G: It's normal.

T: The nervousness?

G: It's gone.

T: Okay, then let's stop here.

With a useful insight and the ANS back to primarily PNS activation, it is safe to end the session. Of course, this trauma is not fully resolved, but resources are in place to further that process. In addition, now that the issue of responsibility has been clarified, the rest of the work should go more easily. A subsequent session with Gail follows in Chapter 8.

CHAPTER SEVEN

Additional Somatic Techniques for Safer Trauma Therapy

DUAL AWARENESS

A normal process among the nontraumatized, dual awareness simply involves being able to maintain awareness of one or more areas of experience simultaneously. As with body awareness, the concept of holding simultaneous awareness of multiple stimuli has its roots in meditation and in gestalt therapy. Here we focus on dual awareness as a prerequisite for safe trauma therapy and as a tool for braking and containment.

PTSD Splits Perception

Most of us are able to strike a balance between the many internal and external sensory stimuli that occupy our awareness at any one time. We are able to notice more than one aspect of our current experience as our focus shifts from one sensation, movement, or activity to another, reconciling physical sensations with respect to our current environment and activity. We are able to shuttle our perceptions from one point of reference to the other, negotiating, compromising, and reconciling the various inputs into a cohesive whole that we term our current "reality." You get a pain in your gut and are able to process that sensation with other information and perceptions you have at hand and remember that you ate too much lunch. In another situation, a similar pain might lead you to the conclusion that you don't like the direction of the current conversation or the tone of someone's voice. A third possibility is that someone just mentioned going to the dentist and you are reminded that it will be your turn tomorrow.

One of the problems that develops in individuals with PTSD is that they become habituated to paying an inordinate amount of attention to internal stimuli and interpreting the world from that point of view. They lose discrimination. Internal sensations become associated with past events, and current reality is evaluated on that restricted information. External perception pales in significance compared to the internal stimuli. The customary reconciliation between what we experience in the body and what we perceive outside of the body is lost. The ability to process multiple stimuli simultaneously becomes diminished. Perception narrows.

This can lead to severe distortions in perceptions of reality and provoke further distress. For example, when a sensation has been associated with the experience of danger (as is the norm with PTSD), perception of any kind of similar sensation may cause one to leap to the conclusion that something dangerous is going on in the environment. There is no regard for other stimuli or information. Anxiety or panic may ensue. As the traumatized individual becomes more and more hypervigilant in an effort to foresee danger, she actually becomes less and less able to identify it. When danger cannot be adequately identified, recognition of safety also becomes impossible. Danger is everywhere, and fear is constant.

I have heard several terms to describe this perceptual split between internal and external sensory stimuli: self and observing ego, core self and witness, child and adult, internal and external reality, etc. However, I prefer the terms coined by van der Kolk, McFarlane, and Weisaeth (1996): the *experiencing self* and the *observing self*.

Developing Dual Awareness

Reconciling this perceptual split is not only necessary to healing trauma but also mandatory for conducting safe trauma therapy. It is not possible for clients to safely address traumatic memories until and unless they are able to maintain a simultaneous awareness and discrimination of past and present. They must be able to know, at least intellectually, that the trauma being addressed is in the past, even though it may *feel* as though it is happening now. Delving into traumatic memory with a client who is unable to maintain this dual awareness risks uncontainable hyperarousal and a possible dive into flashback. This is fertile ground for retraumatization: reexperiencing trauma with all the terror, hopelessness, and desperation first tied to it.

Developing or reconnecting with the facility for dual awareness enables the client to address a trauma while secure in the knowledge that the actual, present environment is trauma-free. It is an extremely useful tool for healing discrepancies between the experiencing and observing selves.

The following client exercise illustrates the difference between the experiencing and the observing selves and demonstrates how to move between the two. This type of exercise can be used with a client before delving into trauma memories. Not only does it give him a chance to practice this new skill, but it is also an indicator of the client's capacity for dual awareness and thereby his readiness to address more difficult material. The instructions are directed to the client.

- *Remember a recent mildly distressing event—something where you were slightly anxious or embarrassed. What do you notice in your body? What happens in your muscles? What happens in your gut? How does your breathing change? Does your heart rate increase or decrease? Do you become warmer or colder? If there is any change in temperature, is it uniform or variable in sectors of your body?*

- *Then bring your awareness back into this room you are in now. Notice the color of the walls, the texture of the rug. What is the temperature of this room? What do you smell here? Does your breathing change as your focus of awareness changes?*

- *Now try to keep awareness of your present surroundings while you remember that slightly distressing event. Is it possible for you to maintain awareness of where you are physically as you remember that event?*

- *End this exercise with your awareness focused on your current surroundings.*

Applying Dual Awareness to Panic and Anxiety Attacks

Acknowledging the split between the experiencing self and the observing self has helped many clients to tolerate being in situations where they are prone to anxiety attacks. A simple technique involves accepting and stating (aloud or in one's thoughts) the reality of *both* the selves simultaneously: "I'm feeling very scared here" (experiencing self's reality), while at the same time actually looking around, evaluating the situation, and saying (if it is true), "*and* I'm not in any actual danger right now " (observing self's reality). It is very important that the conjunction is "and," as that implies a connection between the two phrases; "but" would imply negation of the first phrase. The message is, "Both realities count," not, "There is nothing to be afraid of." Accepting the two perspectives (that of the experiencing self and that of the observing self) simultaneously will often reduce anxiety quickly. It is not clear why this works so well. Perhaps anxiety escalates with nonacceptance of the experiencing self's reality, and when that changes, the whole system relaxes.

Applying Dual Awareness to Flashbacks

It is not advisable to try to resolve PTSD through flashbacks as the experience of a flashback reinforces terror and feelings of helplessness. Psychological tools that were missing to meet the overwhelming trauma are also usually missing to meet the overwhelming flashback; otherwise it would not be a flashback. Integration under those circumstances was and is not possible. Reexperiencing a trauma with the same feelings of helplessness and terror only serves to reinforce its impact. A first step in helping many individuals with PTSD is to teach them to stop and prevent their flashbacks. When flashbacks are under control, it will be possible to equip clients with the resources necessary to meet their traumatic memories on more stable ground. Controlling flashbacks makes it feasible to approach digestible portions of traumatic memories, one at a time.

One problem with flashbacks is that they cannot be predicted. They are difficult to prepare for. They can be triggered anywhere, anytime, even by the therapy setting.

A common therapeutic dilemma occurs when a client goes into flashback during the session, believing the therapy room to be the scene of the trauma and the therapist to be the perpetrator. When this is a regular occurrence, the therapy can be compromised. It is a sign that the client's experiencing self is having free rein, perceiving danger in the place where he is seeking help. The therapist who is perceived as dangerous is not in a position to be helpful.

Under these circumstances, the client's observing self must be awakened and called back into the therapy room, usually with a measure of authority (firm, but not angry) from the therapist: "Look where you are now. What color is the wall here? What color is the rug? What kind of shoes do you have on right now? What is today's date? etc."

When the client's observing self is (again) operational, the following *flashback halting protocol* can be taught. It is based on the principles of dual awareness, reconciling the experiencing self with the observing self. It usually will stop a traumatic flashback quite quickly.

The client says, preferably aloud, the following sentences filling in the blanks and following the instructions:

- Right now I am <u>feeling</u> _____ ,

   (*insert name of the current emotion, usually fear*)
- and I am <u>sensing</u> in my body _____ ,

   (*describe your current bodily sensations—name at least three*),
- because I am <u>remembering</u> _____ .

   (*name the trauma by title, <u>only</u>—no details*).
- <u>At the same time</u>, I am looking around where I am <u>now</u> in _____

   (*the actual current year*),
- here _____ ,

   (*name the place where you are*)
- and I can see _____ ,

   (*describe some of the things that you see right <u>now</u>, in <u>this</u> place*),
- and so I know _____ ,

   (*name the trauma, by title only, again*)
- is not happening now/anymore.

An example:

I was consulted by a therapist whose client had been held hostage in a cellar. Recently she had arrived at her therapist's new office to find it slightly below street level. The superficial similarity of the placement and approach to the new office to the site of the captivity triggered a flashback in the client. It was so strong that

she became terrified of her (otherwise trusted) therapist of two years and consid-
ered termination of treatment—he became associated with her captor. I suggested
that her dual awareness needed to be reestablished—separating the therapist's
new office from the site of the captivity and the therapist from the captor. The
therapist brought this distinction into awareness at the next session, helping the
client to acknowledge the realities of both her experiencing and observing selves.
Using the flashback halting protocol, the client said, "I am feeling very scared of
you because the placement of your new office reminds me of when I was a
hostage, and I got afraid you were my captor. And I can see you right now and
I know you are my therapist. I can also see right now that you are not, nor are
you about to, hurt me. And I know I can leave here any time I want." *The client*
was able to regain her separation of past from present and they were able to con-
tinue the therapeutic relationship and therapy.

The flashback halting protocol can also be effectively adapted for use with
nightmares that may be traumatic flashbacks. This has been used as a ritual
before sleep, to prepare for the expected nightmare:

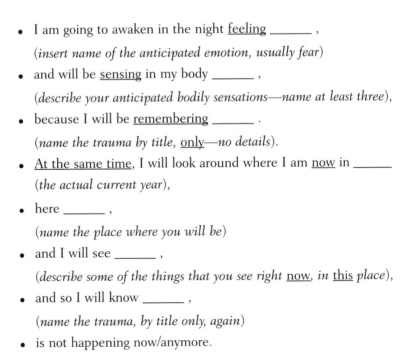

- I am going to awaken in the night <u>feeling</u> _____ ,
  (insert name of the anticipated emotion, usually fear)
- and will be <u>sensing</u> in my body _____ ,
  (describe your anticipated bodily sensations—name at least three),
- because I will be <u>remembering</u> _____ .
  (name the trauma by title, <u>only</u>—no details).
- <u>At the same time,</u> I will look around where I am <u>now</u> in _____
  (the actual current year),
- here _____ ,
  (name the place where you will be)
- and I will see _____ ,
  (describe some of the things that you see right <u>now</u>, in <u>this</u> place),
- and so I will know _____ ,
  (name the trauma, by title only, again)
- is not happening now/anymore.

If the client awakens with a flashback or nightmare, the regular protocol can be used. The client might teach her partner or parent (who ever she is living with) to prompt the protocol, or even state it herself until the client's observing self wakes up.

MUSCLE TONING: TENSION VS. RELAXATION

Chronic muscle contraction underlies what is commonly called "tension." Muscle contraction is not a bad thing; it is necessary to be able to hold ourselves up and for all the movements we make throughout our day. It is also necessary for the development of muscle tone. As previously mentioned, a muscle can only do one thing: contract. When a muscle is not contracting, it is doing what is usually called relaxation. Actually, though, a relaxed muscle is not doing anything.

Muscle tension has come to be regarded as a foe. It seems no one wants to be "tense." People spend a fortune for massages, spas, potions to relax, relax, relax. The positive function of muscle tension is rarely discussed.

Muscle tension is taken for granted; it is often regarded with scorn. It is uncomfortable, so how can it possibly be something good? That muscle tension is a friend is rarely considered. But what would life be like without it? First of all, our bodies would collapse to the ground in a blob of bone and flesh. It is the tension in our muscles that makes it possible for us to stand and sit straight. Muscle tension gives our bodies form, grace, posture, and locomotion. Without muscle tension it would not be possible to perform even the simplest of tasks. Dressing or feeding oneself, holding a pen, playing a sport would not be possible. It is muscle tension that makes possible a baby's first step and the socialization of toilet training. If you are still in doubt, consider muscle-wasting diseases like muscular dystrophy and amyotrophic lateral sclerosis (ALS). They may serve as reminders of just how important muscle tension is. Muscle tension is necessary for daily living.

Certainly there are times when the degree of chronic muscle tension becomes discomforting. And for some, induced relaxation through massage, hot baths, muscle stretching, progressive muscle relaxation, etc. may be very beneficial. However, there are many with PTSD for whom induced relaxation will precipitate a trauma reaction, increasing hyperarousal and anxiety, risking

"He appears to have lost all of his resilience."

© The New Yorker Collection 1987 Arnie Levin from cartoonbank.com. All rights reserved.

flashbacks. There are no studies that discuss this phenomenon; it is an area yet to be researched. However, there are a few articles that mention increases in anxiety in some people due to relaxation-type trainings (Heide & Borkovec, 1983, 1984; Jacobsen & Edinger, 1982; Lehrer & Woolfolk, 1993).

Informal discussion among colleagues suggests that a significant percentage of PTSD clients may become more anxious from relaxation training. In such cases, building or maintaining muscle tension is preferable to relaxation. Simple body awareness is a reliable measure of which is best for a particular client. Clients who become calmer with relaxation can benefit from it. Those who become more anxious when relaxing may be better off tensing instead. There may be a generalized positive or negative response to tensing or relaxation throughout the body. But it is also possible to have a positive experience tensing a particular muscle and a negative experience tensing another (even the same muscle on different sides). Every body is built with different distributions of muscle tone (Bodynamic, 1988–1992). Body awareness is the key to determining when tensing or relaxing a particular muscle benefits or impedes.

It is confusing to think that someone could actually be more relaxed when more tense, an oxymoron. However, it may be that individuals with greater muscle tone are better able to tolerate hyperarousal than those with lesser tone. For instance, a greater degree of muscle tone increases self-confidence and reduces feelings of vulnerability and helplessness.

One consequence of PTSD is body sensations that are very unpleasant. Those that exacerbate feelings of anxiety and panic abound. They usually coincide with autonomic nervous system (ANS) hyperarousal. Some clients describe a peripheral "buzz" just under the skin, as if they had their finger in an electric socket. These unpleasant sensations go hand in hand with the sleep disturbance that so many with PTSD suffer. A common nighttime experience is to feel tired, even sleepy, go to bed and start to relax only to jolt awake with a racing heart and buzzing sensations in the limbs. At that point sleep becomes hopeless for many hours.

Muscle tensing has helped many reduce these unpleasant sensations—even to the point of enabling sleep. The kind of tensing being discussed here does not include aerobic exercise. That is contraindicated for some individuals with PTSD and panic attacks, as the elevated heart and respiration rates can be trauma triggers in themselves. Rather, it is slow, focused, muscle-building exercise that is beneficial in these circumstances. For this kind of muscle building to be effective, it must be done with body awareness—with attention to body sensations generally and to the muscles being exercised specifically (Bodynamic, 1988–1992). Also, the exercise must stop at the point of mild tiredness in the muscle, while it is still a pleasant experience. Doing repetitions "till you feel the burn" is not helpful for building muscle tone that aids emotional containment. Exercises that enhance sensations of calm, solidity, and increased presence are beneficial. Any that bring anxiety, nausea, disorientation, etc., are not. The idea is to build a positive experience of being in the body by developing musculature that can better contain hyperarousal and the full range of the emotions. A further goal is to build a positive experience of being in the body so that the desire to reside in the body and continue the exercise develops. In that way it becomes self-rewarding.

Joanie was intimately aware of her need for muscle tension. She had been vulnerable and impulsive as a young adult, prone to drifting from project to project. She had trouble keeping a job and was subject to periodic bursts of anger as well as a general level of anxiety. Moving to a country where bicycle riding was a major form of transportation turned out to be a blessing for her. As she got used to riding great distances, her legs became stronger and stronger, and, amazingly, she grew more and more stable—all this before she ever considered psychotherapy. She was very aware of the role increased muscle tone in her thighs had in her newfound ability to maintain her focus and contain her emotions. However, when she was ill or visiting family in another country and unable to ride for a while, her previous instability would creep back.

A simple toning exercise to begin with is push-ups. They build tone in the backs of the arms (triceps), the chest (pectorals), and the back (trapezius and rhomboids). They can also be done at home with no special equipment. It is easiest to begin standing a few feet from a wall, leaning into it and pushing away. Gradually one can move lower on the wall until there is enough strength to push off from stairs or the floor. Leg lifts in many directions (quadriceps, tensor fascia lata, hamstrings, and gluteals) also need no special equipment. Cheap free weights, milk cartons, or books can be used for strengthening the front of the upper arms (biceps).

In addition to increasing general emotional stability, muscle tensing is used by some as an emergency measure when anxiety threatens to escalate into overwhelming anxiety or panic. Below are a few postures that can be used to tense specific muscles. Most people will find at least one of them an aid to on-the-spot containment. Of course, any postures that increase anxiety should not be used.

Tensing Peripheral Muscles—Holding Together

Important: Any tensing should be done only until the muscle feels slightly tired. Release of the tensing must be done slowly. This is not progressive muscle relaxation. The idea here is to try to maintain a little of the contraction/tension. Try one exercise and evaluate with body awareness before going on to the next. If tensing causes any adverse reaction (nausea, spacyness, anxiety, etc.), you can usually neutralize that reaction by gently stretching the same muscle—making an opposite movement (Bodynamic, 1988–1992).

- *Side of Legs*: Stand with feet a little less than shoulder-width apart, knees relaxed (neither locked, nor bent). Press knees out directly to the side so that you can feel tension along the sides of the legs from knee to hip (Bodynamic, 1988–1992).

- *Left arm*: Sit or stand with arms crossed right over left. The right hand should be covering the left elbow. First, the right hand provides resistance as the left arm lifts directly away from the body. You should feel tension in the forward-directed part of the upper arm from shoulder to elbow. Next, the right hand provides resistance to the back of the elbow as the left arm pushes directly left. You should feel tension in the left-directed part of the upper arm from shoulder to elbow (Robyn Bohen, personal communication, 1991).

- *Right arm*: Sit or stand with arms crossed left over right. The left hand should be covering the right elbow. First, the left hand provides resistance as the right arm lifts directly away from the body. You should feel tension in the forward-directed part of the upper arm from shoulder to elbow. Next, the left hand provides resistance to the back of the elbow as the right arm pushes directly right. You should feel tension in the right-directed part of the upper arm from shoulder to elbow (Robyn Bohen, personal communication, 1991).

- *Thighs*: Sitting in a chair, place both feet flat on the floor. Press weight onto your feet just until you feel tension build in your thighs.

Muscle tensing became the foundation of therapy with one client:

Theresa was in her mid thirties when she began seeing me. She suffered from PTSD and borderline personality disorder. She was not very functional and was unable to work. She had difficulty setting goals—she was either empty of ideas or full of pipe dreams. Early in my work with Theresa she expressed the desire to someday be able to hold a steady job, get married, and raise a family. I affirmed her desire but commented that we couldn't achieve it that day. "What," I asked, "is one thing you can do today that is a small step toward those goals?" After considering this she surprised me by saying, "I need backbone." She meant it both figuratively and literally. Upon closer inquiry, I found out that she felt very weak in her back and could not, in fact, feel the support of her spine. That day we began strengthening Theresa's spinal muscles through slow exercise, using body awareness. I would have her slump in her usual posture, then slowly straighten up, becoming taller. We kept the pace slow, so that she could keep up with the change in muscle tension and monitor other body sensations. I was particularly interested in her noticing where she was having to tense up to sit up. It was hard work. She repeated the movement several times—slump, straighten, slump, straighten. The exercise became homework. In subsequent sessions we regularly referred to her newly developed spinal tension—her "backbone." Gradually, it became a dependable support and resource for her—both literally and figuratively—as she traversed some of the difficult themes in her life.

PHYSICAL BOUNDARIES

Boundaries are of many kinds. This section will focus on discussion of *interpersonal* and *concrete* boundaries that are associated with the body.

Interpersonal Boundaries

If you have ever "known" someone was standing behind you before you turned to look, or felt the person you were talking to was standing too close, you have perceived an interpersonal boundary. It is not a mysterious or mystical line, but something quite palpable that is often experienced at various distances. Your interpersonal boundary circumscribes what you feel to be your personal space. One interpersonal boundary is that point at which the distance between you and another turns from comfortable to uncomfortable. Another kind is what animal behaviorists call *critical distance*, the point at which a wild animal turns from cautious alert to attack. Determining a boundary's distance is not only very individual but also dependent on the situation. What might be an uncomfortable distance at a particular time or with a particular person might well be quite comfortable at another time or with someone else, and vice versa.

Therapeutic Distance

Sometimes a problem develops during therapy that seems to have no origin and no solution. The following consultation illustrates a problem that has occurred both with seasoned therapists and with therapists in training. Although a bit extreme, the situation described here is not unusual. In this instance, the client was becoming ill—headaches and vomiting—within a few hours after each therapy session. The therapist and client could not identify a cause, and both were concerned.

I met with therapist and client together. First I was briefed on the client's personal history and the history of the therapy. As the therapist worked a lot with the body, I ventured that perhaps the body work was too provoking and rigorous for the client. No, they did no body work at all; they just talked. Okay. Well then, might the material being discussed be too traumatic, too much for the client, too provocative? No, they were only discussing issues from the client's daily life. Since the problem was not in the content or method, I became curious about the phys-ical arrangements. How did they usually sit together? They showed me by placing themselves facing each other in chairs approximately one meter apart.

I asked the client to scan for body awareness and report any sensations. The client felt a rapid heart rate, cold sweaty hands, and slight nausea. I suggested that the client move back and see what happened. He felt a slight relief. I encouraged him to find a distance and a placement that further reduced the discomforting symptoms. He moved back further and to the side. There was more relief, but the client was still a bit uncomfortable. The client continued to experiment in this way. Finally, a placement of chairs about three meters apart, turned diagonally so they were no longer facing each other, gave a lot of relief—all signs of sympathetic arousal, were replaced by signs of parasympathetic arousal.

The client did not become ill after that consultation. Both client and therapist continued to pay close attention to their sitting position in subsequent sessions, and the client had no further problem with illness following therapy sessions.

Two Exercises to Explore Boundaries*

While the following exercises will be familiar to many, they are worth includ-ing for those who have not encountered them before.

---

* The history of these exercises is curious as there are several organizations that claim to have originated each. Either the original inspiration for them has been long forgotten, or those groups have coincidentally developed similar exercises at around the same time.

The first interpersonal boundary exercise is done in pairs. One partner slowly walks toward the other. The stationary partner keeps track of her own body sensations and says "stop" when she begins to feel uncomfortable. It is a good idea to repeat the exercise several times with the stationary partner standing at different angles to the moving partner—face, right and left shoulder, back toward the walking partner. It is important that the stationary partner talks about what she senses in her body and feelings.

This exercise illustrates the difficulty many have feeling their boundary and being able to say "no" or "stop." Sometimes the stationary partner's body and emotional state never change, so she never says "stop" and the moving partner ends up walking into her. When this happens it is usually because the starting distance was already inside of the stationary partner's interpersonal boundary. *It is not possible for the stationary partner to feel her boundary when the moving partner is already past it at the start point.* If this happens, try repeating the exercise from a greater start distance. This is also true for people in their daily lives. It is not possible to feel where your "stop" or "no" point is if you have already crossed it. So if a client reports that the distance between the two of you is okay, consider if the client is actually comfortable or if she can't feel her boundary because you are already too close. When in doubt, have either of you move a little and see what happens. You can always move back to where you started. An example:

As we began our second session, Thomas looked like he was holding his breath. I inquired about our placement. He said it was fine, but still did not breathe. I suggested I move back a little just to see what happened and he agreed. When I did he immediately exhaled and breathed easier. He also noticed the change. We proceeded with the session from that distance.

The second interpersonal boundary exercise involves the use of yarn (or string or rope) to help visualize one's boundary. The client in individual therapy or in a group therapy takes a length of yarn and uses it to draw a circle around himself at the radius he perceives his comfort distance to be. It is good to have the client talk about the experience while he is doing it, including how it feels in his body to make his boundary concrete. Then, with the client's permission, the therapist can roam about the room moving in and out of the client's boundary (as we actually do with others all the time). The client is asked to track his somatic and emotional responses, expressing what is happening while the therapist walks. He should notice when he feels an unmolested space, and when he feels intruded on. He should also feel free to adjust his boundary at any time. A point worthy of note: The wider the radius of the boundary, the more easily it is invaded and the more frequent and intense the client's feelings of intrusion. Eventually, the client can be taught to redraw his boundary (actually with the yarn, as well as figuratively).

When the client is ready, an additional intervention can be useful: With the client's permission the therapist comes to a pause just inside the client's yarn and does not move. The client will usually feel uncomfortable, sometimes angry. The therapist then helps the client to figure out that if he draws his boundary in a tighter circle around him, the therapist will no longer be intruding inside of his boundary. Often this gives a client a feeling of mastery over his personal space that he can take out into his daily life in business, social, and personal contacts, on public transportation, in restaurants, etc.

Concrete Boundary at the Skin Level

The expression "thin skinned" is apt in describing many with PTSD. Traumatic events often intrude past the skin, either physically or psychologically.

A 3-year-old friend of mine, Lane, had suffered plenty of medical trauma. She greatly enjoyed the company of one child at a time, but was unable to tolerate the stimulation of multiple children. At an annual family gathering she clung desperately to one or the other of her parents. Though she was usually secure with their comfort, this time it was not enough for her as the excitement generated by several children increased.

I was touched by her plight and carefully approached her as she held fast to her mother, visibly shaken. I took my hand and began to gently, but firmly, rub the surface of her back. As I did this I said, "Here's Lane. Can you feel Lane here?"

She began to calm and relax. Her whimpering ceased. As long as I kept my hand at her back, reminding her of where her physical body was, and where it stopped, she could maintain her composure. Whenever I withdrew my hand, her upset would again increase, even if I continued the verbal reminders. Her mother and I were both fascinated at the dramatic change when I marked her boundary, and disturbed that she couldn't maintain it in the absence of my hand. Later that week Lane's mother and I discussed strategies for increasing her sense of physical boundary. We invented games they could play together. One involved their placing hands, arms, legs, or feet together and mom instructing Lane to shift the focus of the sensations at the surface of her skin: "Feel Mommy, now feel Lane." As such exercises helped Lane to have a more secure sense of the edges of her body, her tolerance of child uproar improved.

Thickening Helen's Skin

Helen was in her mid-twenties when she sought therapy following a childhood marred by sexual and physical abuse. Needless to say, she had many problems and was very "thin skinned." A city dweller without a car, she was often plagued with anxiety when confronted with public transportation. It wasn't the travel itself that was intimidating, but the risk of inadvertent physical contact. Her fear of casual touch was evident even in the therapy situation. She needed to be very careful as she entered and left my room lest we accidentally brushed shoulders. She made me promise I would never give her an affectionate pat on the shoulder on her way out the door. I'd never had a client so fearful of even bumping shoulders with someone.

As my first principle is attending to the safety of the client both in and outside of the session, I proposed that we figure out a way to help her feel in control of casual touch—to give her some tools to avoid it, stop it, and keep it from feeling like it invaded beneath her skin. We both knew that bumping into people was sometimes inevitable on buses, trains, and subways.

First Helen worked on building muscle tone to thicken and toughen the cushioning under her skin. Highly motivated, she lifted weights, did push-ups and sit-ups and walked daily for several months. Next we constructed a program whereby she could learn to move away from an unwanted touch or move the hand or shoulder of another away from her. She was convinced she needed to become proficient at this and was willing to brave some discomfort to achieve it.

In this instance I made an exception to my rule of not touching trauma clients, as the program we created necessitated brief touch. Helen insisted that the potential gains outweighed the risks. (An option would have been to encourage her to try the same exercises with a trusted friend, or have her bring a friend to the therapy. That would bypass the therapist-client touch issue. However, Helen had no friends at the time we embarked on this task—she was too afraid of being touched to have any.)

Helen chose the initial task. I would demonstrate first; then she would try herself. We stood, facing each other at arm's length, and when she was ready, she would place her hand on my shoulder. Then I would twist my trunk away from her hand and step back out of reach, causing her hand to fall to her side. When it was Helen's turn, she would tell me when she was ready for me to place my hand on her shoulder. She would then try a similar twist with a back step until my arm fell at my side.

Next we tried standing shoulder to shoulder. I instructed her first to just try stepping to the side away from my shoulder. Once she had that down I suggested she stay where she was and just pull her shoulders in toward the center of her body, narrowing her shoulder width, so that the distance between our shoulders increased.

This may seem very simplistic, but for Helen it was very hard work. She had a lot of anxiety at first, but as her facility grew she became calmer and more confident.

Our third exercise involved standing facing at arm's length again. Helen would ask me to place my hand on her shoulder; then she would remove it more directly. One way was to just push it with the opposite hand; another was to rotate the arm on the same side in a circle, gently batting my arm away. We discussed the importance of doing this calmly, even if she were angry. The idea was to stop someone from touching her, not to provoke a conflict.

We drilled these exercises again and again over many weeks. As Helen's facility grew, her "skin" seemed to toughen and thicken and with that her confidence to venture out in the world increased. She also became more trusting of me, as she felt more capable of stopping me from doing something she didn't want. Eventually she eased her vigilance. One day she surprised me by asking me to change my promise. Now she wanted me to casually touch her as she entered and left my room—a pat on the shoulder or the like. She wanted to see how it felt and decide herself if she would accept the touch or move away from it.

Establishing a Sense of Boundary at the Skin Level

Trauma and PTSD are often the result of events that were in one way or another physically invasive: assault, rape, car accidents, surgery, torture, beatings, etc. Often it is loss of the sense of bodily integrity that accelerates a trauma process out of control. Reestablishing the sense of boundary at the skin level will often reduce hyperarousal and increase the feeling of control over one's own body. To increase the sense of bodily integrity, I often suggest that a client physically feel his/her periphery/boundary—the skin. This can be done in several ways:

1. Have your client use his own hands to rub firmly (not too light, not too hard) over his entire surface. Make sure the rubbing stays on the surface—skin (clothes over skin)—and does *not* become a gripping or massaging of muscles. If your client doesn't like touching himself, he can use a wall or door (often a cold wall is great) to rub against a pillow or towel to make the contact. Remember, especially, the back and the sides of the arms and legs.

2. Some clients will feel too provoked even touching their own skin or being observed doing it. In that case it might work to have them sense their skin through sensing the objects they are in contact with. Have the person feel where his buttocks meet the chair, his feet meet the inside of his shoes, the palms of his hands rest on his thighs, etc.

3. As the client does one of these, it is sometimes also useful to have him saying to himself, "This is me," "This is where I stop," etc.

Visual Boundaries

For some clients, just having the therapist look at them is an intrusion. Reactions can be strong. Often intense feelings of shame or embarrassment underlie this difficulty. In such cases it can be a fairly simple matter for the therapist to turn her gaze away. Clients with this difficulty will be greatly relieved when the therapist looks away. It takes some getting used to for the therapist who is accustomed to relying on visual cues, but the potential benefit to the client should help the therapist to tolerate her discomfort.

THE QUESTION OF CLIENT-THERAPIST TOUCH

There is no denying the universal need for touch and human contact. This is no less true for the traumatized—perhaps more so. However, there can be complications when the need for touch is met in the therapeutic situation. Both transference and countertransference can be provoked to an uncontainable degree. For more stable clients (Type I and Type IIA), the hazards may be minimized, but with Type IIB clients therapist touch is too risky to be advisable. For example, it is not unusual for the touching therapist to become perceived as a perpetrator to the physically or sexually abused client. Needless to say, this is not helpful to the therapeutic process. Here is an example of learning the hard way:

Kurt had been both abused and neglected in his developmental years. He demanded a lot of my time and attention. I encouraged Kurt to increase his body awareness and learn his interpersonal boundaries, but he was skeptical. During several sessions he complained of needing to be held. He was sure that was what he needed from me. He became angry when I hesitated. He finally insisted that we just try it and see how it went. Going against my better judgment, I relented. He wanted me to put my arms around him as we sat side by side on the couch. Instead of experiencing the relieving contact he envisioned, his anxiety climbed. He couldn't relax and became frustrated with himself, and then with me. He felt that I must have been doing something wrong because he was feeling so scared. Kurt was not able to connect his rising fear at being held now with his earlier history of abuse; I became perceived as the perpetrator. It was not possible to resolve the conflict during subsequent sessions and he eventually left therapy with me.

A better strategy for helping the traumatized client to get her needs for touch met is to teach her how to meet those needs among her closest family and friends or in a group therapy situation. For a client to be able to ask for, receive, and utilize touch among her network, she must have developed the ability to perceive and respect her own boundaries.

As a consequence of years of incest, Blair was confused about her boundaries. She knew she needed contact and often went beyond what was comfortable for her to get it. She was often promiscuous in an effort to get physical contact. In the past she had suffered several bouts of sexually transmitted diseases. It was a confusing dilemma for her: If she respected her interpersonal boundary she was afraid she would never again be touched. She knew no compromise. After helping her to increase her body awareness, I suggested that she run an experiment at home. She agreed. I advised that she choose a friend, male or female, with whom she could experiment with her touch boundaries. We discussed the pros and cons of several choices; Blair settled on two people she would ask. When one friend agreed, I coached Blair in the experiment. Blair would monitor her body awareness throughout and record the changes for us to discuss at the next session.

The experiment involved Blair's finding out what kind of touch her friend could give while Blair maintained a normal heart rate and breathing—that is, did not become anxious. At first Blair thought the experiment was a bit ludicrous. She was so used to being touched that she was skeptical that she needed such caution. But she found out differently. When she focused on her sensations, she discovered that she did indeed become anxious when she was held around her whole body. It was the first time she realized that her promiscuous behavior necessitated cutting off from her body sensations. Through pursuing the experiment, she further discovered that hand holding was completely comfortable. In the ensuing weeks, Blair paid more attention to her body awareness when she was being touched. In the therapy sessions, we looked at her discoveries and she received further coaching on how to ask for the kind of touch she wanted and how to say no to touch she didn't want.

MITIGATING SESSION CLOSURE

Every trauma therapist knows that ending a single trauma therapy session can sometimes be difficult; as discussed previously, trauma processes can easily accelerate. When timing of a session does not fit within the usual therapeutic time frame, it can be difficult for both therapist and client. Most of the principles and techniques discussed in this and the preceding two chapters can be used as aids to easing the problem of session closure. They can be applied both to pace the session and to end it.

Equipping the client to apply the brakes gives an advantage to both client and therapist. For the client, the safety of the therapeutic process is increased as he gains confidence in his ability to control—turn on and turn off—his traumatic memories. Courage to confront difficult issues usually increases when the client knows he can come out of it any time. When client and therapist are well practiced in braking before traumatic material is addressed, acceleration can be stopped at any time. Further, keeping the client's arousal at a low level throughout the therapy session assures that the process will not get out of control in the first place. Familiarity with the client's resources will help the therapist keep the client from processes where he does not have the tools to stop. Of course, there will be times when judgment slips and the session will need to be extended a few minutes for the purpose of putting on the brakes, but this will not occur often if the preparation is adequate.

Sometimes the best strategy to timing session closure is to end early. It can be useful to be on the look-out for "stopping places" (as with Gail's session at the end of the previous chapter)—an integration, an "aha!," a spontaneous reduction in arousal. There are often several within a single session. It is usually better to send the client home after a briefer session where he reached a significant integration or relief than to continue the session to the end of the allotted time when he may be uncomfortable or in a muddle. The time left after stopping specific trauma work can also be well used to address integration of trauma therapy into the client's daily life.

In the next chapter, application of body awareness and other somatic tools will be discussed in relationship to facilitating the addressing of traumatic memories.

CHAPTER EIGHT

Somatic Memory Becomes Personal History

Regardless of the techniques or modalities employed, the goals of trauma therapy should be:

1. To unite implicit and explicit memories into a comprehensive narrative of the events and aftermath of the traumatic incident. This includes making sense of body sensations and behaviors within that context.
2. To eliminate symptoms of ANS hyperarousal in connection with those memories.
3. To relegate the traumatic event to the past: "It is over. That was a long time ago. I survived."

Since the mid-1980s several treatment models for working with trauma have emerged. In fact, within the field a feeling of competition has arisen. The prevailing expectation is for one therapy model to emerge as *the* therapy for trauma. This attitude is cause for concern, because it does a disservice to our clients. Each available therapy helps some clients, and each of them also fails at times. Every modality has strengths as well as weaknesses. Just as there is no one medication to treat anxiety or depression, there is no one-size-fits-all trauma therapy. In fact, sometimes it is the therapeutic relationship, not any technique or model, that is the primary force for healing trauma. All of the trauma treatment modalities, though, have two things in common: They are all highly structured, and they are all highly directive. Each method involves a precise protocol that must be followed to reach resolution of traumatic memories. This requires that the therapist be directive, steering the protocol rather than following the client's process. It appears that this commonality is no accident. Those working with trauma—from divergent disciplines—demonstrate agreement that working with trauma requires structure and direction. This makes sense as following the client's process without intervention usually results in either avoidance of traumatic memories or becoming overwhelmed by them.

Though efficacy studies can help point the way to suitable models, they can also be misleading. First of all, most such studies are based on Type I trauma clients. In addition, studies conducted by the proponents of one method primarily report positive results, whereas those conducted by opponents report negative results. Perhaps a better basis for judging the success or failure of a method might be to trust the client's body awareness and symptom profile: "Has this helped you? Are you calmer, more contained, better functioning? Okay, let's continue." "This isn't helping? You feel worse, more unstable, less able to handle your daily life? Okay, let's try something else." As previously stated, the safest trauma therapy comprises several models, so the therapy can be adapted to the specific needs of the client.

Regardless of the therapy methods that are being employed, the topics presented in this chapter will be fundamental to improving the quality and outcome of trauma therapy.

BEWARE THE WRONG ROAD

Memory is malleable and subject to influence. Continuous as well as recovered memories can be highly accurate, and they can also have inaccuracies. A good illustration of the vulnerability of memory is provided by a friend's son who broke his arm at the age of 8. The boy, now 12, remembers most of the incident accurately: falling from the tree, breaking the arm, the trip to the hospital, having the arm set by a doctor. However, there is one integral detail that he misremembers. In the boy's memory it is his mother who held him as the broken bone was set. Actually, it was his father. The implications of this kind of memory distortion are profound. A continuous or recovered memory of an incidence of abuse could, for example, be generally true, while the perpetrator, or age, or place, etc., could be remembered inaccurately. This is not to say that all recovered memories should be suspect; it is also possible for them to be highly accurate, as has been shown in studies and reports by Andrews (1997), Duggal and Sroufe (1998), and Williams (1995).

The uncertain nature of memory forces the trauma therapist into a difficult position. Clients present memories of trauma that have been continuous; they also present memories that have been recalled as a part of therapy, outside of therapy, and even prior to therapy. Memories can also be recalled whether or not you or the client are attempting to recover them. No matter how the memories occur, the problem remains. How does one evaluate the accuracy of a memory? When there are corroborative records, witnesses, or evidence, the veracity of memory can be determined. When there is no corroboration, accuracy may be suspect. It may not be possible to determine the correctness of a "memory."

A therapeutic dilemma occurs when either the therapist and/or the client feels a need to credit an unsubstantiated memory as "true" or "false." Onno Van der Hart and Ellert Nijenhuis (1999) call this "reflexive belief" and caution against its practice as the risk of false negatives or false positives is high. Whichever attribution, true or false, is applied, it will greatly influence the direction of the therapy and the client's life. The only route under such circumstances is to continue the work but restrain the judgment. That can be difficult to bear for both client and therapist. But not to do so risks making a mistake with dire consequences.

Risks Along the Wrong Road

It is easy to get led down the wrong road. When that happens, the client can suffer greatly. Decompensation can even occur. Of course, it is not always possible to tell if decompensation is the result of the impact of a recovered traumatic memory or destabilization from seeking the memory of a trauma that is not there. When in doubt, signs of hyperarousal in the autonomic nervous system as well as other symptoms, are good indicators. An example:

Brad came to therapy depressed, anxious, and suicidal. He was pale, his breathing quick and shallow. This, he reported, was not his normal mode. He became increasingly decompensated while seeing another psychotherapist whom he had engaged after developing feelings of having been raped as a child. The therapist had been working with him to recover memories of a possible childhood rape. When Brad became seriously suicidal, he realized something was wrong and went looking for another therapist.

Brad's childhood had been troubled. He was arrested a couple of times as a juvenile and had spent several months in detention. This background became pertinent in accessing Brad's current state. Approximately nine months prior to his engaging the other psychotherapist, Brad's house had been burglarized and ransacked while he was out one evening with his family; the burglar had set off a silent alarm. Brad arrived home to find his house crawling with police. The previous therapist had not paid attention to that disturbing, recent incident at all, but had headed straight for the felt, but unknown rape. Brad proceeded to decompensate more and more as they looked further for childhood memories to explain the feeling of rape.

After I took Brad's history I said to him, "You may or may not have been raped as a child. There is no way to know as you do not remember and there are no records. However, the fact of the recent burglary and subsequent police intrusion is enough to account for your symptoms, your feelings of having been raped. Many people would describe their reaction to such an intrusion as 'feeling as if I have been raped.' If you factor in your juvenile arrest record, I can imagine that both the burglary and the police intrusion were very shocking for you."

Upon hearing my evaluation, Brad visibly calmed. Healthy color crept into his cheeks. His respiration deepened and slowed. The decrease in arousal was palpable in the room; Brad could feel it distinctly in his body. His suicidal ideation disappeared. Within the week he was emotionally contained and back to a normal level of functioning. In subsequent sessions, we addressed those more recent events.

Unfortunately, this is not an isolated example. One way to avoid this kind of therapeutic error is to take a careful history and always ask, "What brings you into therapy *now?*" If the answer is something like "a suspicion" of early abuse or other forms of trauma, always ask further, "What brought that up now?" or "What triggered that now?" If the client isn't sure, careful questioning about stressful events within the last few months to a year may lead to a triggering incident that needs to be addressed first. Focusing on the current event that brought a client to therapy in the first place is one way to avoid going down the wrong road.

Getting All the Information

An excellent example of avoiding a wrong road by getting all the pertinent information is provided by Donald Nathanson in the first chapter of *Shame and Pride* (1992). Nathanson used common sense that saved his client a lot of money and a lot of anguish. He describes a former patient who returned for therapy confounded that he had lost his capacity for dealing with his anxiety, something his previous therapy had emphasized. His current high level of anxiety was impervious to all of the tools he had gained. He was "afraid of everything." At the first interview, among other information-gathering, Nathanson wisely questioned the patient's "nasal speech" and found out he had been suffering a cold. It turned out that the client was taking medication that contained pseudoephedrine, a kind of synthetic adrenaline. Such medications mimic the body's reaction to stress—heightened sympathetic arousal. It quickly became clear to Nathanson that this patient's symptoms were caused by the medication, not by anxiety. Relieving the anxiety symptoms then became easy—just change the medication.

Imagine what would have happened to Nathanson's patient if this doctor had not been so wise. They would have begun to look for a psychological cause for his anxiety, digging and digging. The results could have been disastrous as well as costly. Such mistakes are easily made when either a therapist or client acts on preconceived predictions and leaps to psychological causes for somatic symptoms. Severe problems can occur when the preconceived leap is to trauma.

Other physical conditions can mimic psychological problems. For example, consider the hormonal changes due to aging. *Perimenopause* is the term now being applied to the extended period of hormonal and menstrual changes that lead up to the menopause, the complete cessation of menstruation. Perimenopause can begin as many as ten years before actual menopause. During that time hormones may fluctuate erratically and create numerous physical and psychological symptoms (Begley, 1999), including ones that mimic anxiety.

Dorothy, 48, would awaken suddenly in the night feeling very warm, her heart racing. Influenced by a friend who was in therapy and a self-help book she had read, she began to wonder if she had been molested as a child and was starting to have disturbing dreams. She was very upset. I suspected her symptoms might be consistent with perimenopausal changes. She was not waking with a sweaty hot flash, but something similar. Because she still had regular periods, she had not considered that her symptoms could be hormone related. I suggested that she keep a log of the pattern of the night-time incidents and referred her to her gynecologist for hormone tests. Both the tests and the log confirmed that these incidents occurred cyclically, when estrogen levels were the lowest. Her anxiety over possible molestation disappeared.

One further caution: The effects of early medical trauma can be mistaken for effects of physical and sexual abuse. Medical intervention that involves genital or anal areas—surgery, examinations, treatment of vaginal or bladder infections, rectal thermometers, suppositories, and enemas—can be traumatic for some children. As adults, the somatic symptoms can mimic those of sexual abuse. It is important to consider possible medical trauma when evaluating adults with unconfirmed suspicions of child physical or sexual abuse.

It is critical to consider more than the client's belief or the therapist's intuition of the cause of symptoms. Careful and comprehensive history-taking, as well as a generous dose of common sense, will go a long way to prevent potentially damaging excursions down the wrong road.

SEPARATING PAST FROM PRESENT

Ultimately, the main goal of trauma therapy is to relegate the trauma to its rightful place in the client's past. For that, explicit memory processes must be engaged to secure the context of the event in time and space. Usually separation of past and present is an automatic result of any good trauma therapy; it does not usually need to be addressed head-on. The following example is an exception. It is included here to emphasize the importance of recognizing a trauma is over, past, done, and survived. In this unusual instance, that message sank in with only one intervention. It is not likely to happen in the normal course of trauma therapy, though it is what we are striving for.

Usually anxious in a group, Dorte became panicked during a workshop exercise (racing heart, dry mouth, cold sweat). Through simple attention to body awareness, a memory emerged. As a child Dorte had been trapped by a group of other youngsters who taunted and restrained her. She had been very frightened. She kept repeating to me, "I couldn't get away, I couldn't get away." Each time she repeated the phrase her hyperarousal increased both to my observation and by Dorte's report. In an attempt to circumvent this rise, I commented, "But you did get away. I know you got away." Her symptoms continued and she became confused. I asked her if she would like to know how I knew she got away. She nodded vigorously, yes, she did. Pointing to the place where she was sitting I responded simply, "I know you got away because you are here." "Oh!" she replied—and I could almost see the light bulb go on over her head. She comprehended immediately that she could not be sitting in front of me if she had not, indeed, gotten away. Her symptoms of panic disappeared simultaneously with that insight and did not return. She was still not wild about being in groups, but her extreme anxiety decreased considerably following that intervention.

Separating past from present can also be accomplished on a body level. Sometimes an intervention as simple as encouraging a client to move a finger or an arm or just get up and walk while working with a traumatic memory will help to reinforce the here-and-now reality that the trauma is no longer occurring: I could not move then, but I can move now.

WORKING WITH THE AFTERMATH OF THE TRAUMA FIRST

It is a mistake to consider a single traumatic incident as a solitary event. Every traumatic event is comprised of three distinct stages, any one of which can increase or decrease the ultimate impact of trauma. The three stages are: (1) circumstances leading up to the traumatic incident, (2) the traumatic incident itself, and (3) the circumstances following the incident, both short-term (minutes and hours) and long-term (days, weeks, months).

before the trauma → the actual traumatic event → after the trauma

The time following a traumatic event is critical. The quality of contact and help the victim receives can greatly influence the outcome. It is for this reason that it is often advisable to resolve the issues following a traumatic incident first, before attempting to address the incident itself. Sometimes what occurs after the incident is more emotionally devastating than the incident itself. Imagine, for example, the potential outcomes for the trauma victims in the following scenarios:

1. Two women with corresponding backgrounds and personalities are similarly injured in the same type of car accident.

A's husband arrives at the hospital visibly shaken, worried about his wife's condition. He greets her warmly and with obvious concern.

B's husband arrives at the hospital angry. He is worried about the condition of the new, expensive car. He greets his wife with accusation.

2. Two war veterans also with corresponding backgrounds and personalities are from the same combat unit. They are both discharged following injuries received during the same offensive.

In his community A is welcomed home as a hero. Everyone is concerned about his injuries. He is given help to reestablish himself.

B, on the other hand, is greeted by his friends with contempt for his violent acts. His family is impatient that his recovery seems slow. He is not given help to reestablish himself in his community.

It does not take a research study to speculate that, all other variables being equal, the As in the above scenarios are likely to fare better than the Bs. Just as a tidal wave sometimes follows an earthquake, the aftermath of trauma can wreak even greater damage.

Regardless of the treatment method, choosing which part of a traumatic incident is to be addressed first can be critical to the course and outcome of the therapy. Approaching direct work with traumatic memories is always difficult. When started from the beginning of the event, the load can be insurmountable:

before the trauma → the actual traumatic event + after the trauma

Start at the beginning, and there is all of it to face.

One of the wisdoms of addressing the circumstances that came after the trauma first is that it reduces the load considerably when addressing the actual incident. Afterward, when approaching the actual event, there is only that to contend with:

before the trauma → the actual traumatic event ‖ ~~after the trauma~~

Moreover, when you start at the end, the client gets to face the worst of the traumatic event secure in the knowledge that it did actually end, and she has survived.

The following case, illustrates these points:

Ruth* is a Western European woman in her mid-thirties who at 19 was raped during a student vacation in a Middle Eastern country. She works as a social worker for immigrants and often comes in contact with refugees from the Middle East. She sought therapy after noticing that over the previous few months she had growing anxiety at work, which was beginning to interfere with her ability to continue her job. She was experiencing increasing flashbacks of the rape, difficulty concentrating, and periodic nightmares.

The therapy began with my taking a careful case history. As we discussed her past and current situation, it became clear that her current anxiety had been set off after she had been threatened by one of her Middle Eastern clients several months earlier. She hadn't thought much about it at the time, but could now see the connection. She was a Type I client with no other incidence of sexual assault or other trauma in her history. We discussed Ruth's situation at work and she agreed that for the time being she would not work with potentially violent clients—she was already receiving support for this from her colleagues.

Early in therapy Ruth outlined the circumstances surrounding the rape. She had been traveling with a group of friends, but had chosen to go off by herself one day with a polite young Arab, Abdul, who offered to show her the city. No one thought much about it. Abdul was very knowledgeable and showed her many places she wouldn't have otherwise seen. Toward the end of the day they encountered one of Abdul's friends and went back to Abdul's apartment. As night fell, she was told by Abdul that he would have sex with her but would not allow his friend to because Abdul was "in love" with her. She protested and asked to be taken back to her hotel. Abdul threatened that if she didn't allow him, both of them would have sex with her. Ruth then went dead in her body. The next morning Abdul showed her back to her hotel, stopping to buy her breakfast on the way. When they arrived, her friends expressed

---

* This case example is extracted and condensed from a previously published article (Rothschild, 1996/7, 1997).

concern about where she had been, but Ruth was so embarrassed and ashamed about what had happened that she told them she had spent the night dancing.

Once home, a vaginal infection forced Ruth to seek medical treatment. A gynecologist was the first person she told about the rape. His response was cold and clinical, with an edge of sexual interest that increased her feeling of shame. Eventually she told one of the friends she had traveled with. She remembered feeling ashamed and fearing she would be judged. Her friend, however, was very compassionate, terribly sorry for what had happened. Ruth felt relieved to have finally told someone.

Over several sessions early in the therapy we decided to take a look at the situation immediately following the actual rape. Here the connections to her inability to act against the offender or seek help gradually became clear.

When Ruth and Abdul left his apartment the next morning, Ruth felt she had to be nice to him. She didn't know where she was or how to get to her hotel. She couldn't speak the language. She felt dependent on Abdul to get her back to safety—dependent for safety on the man who had raped her! So she let him hold her right hand. As she remembered, she could feel the tension in that hand and the impulse to draw it away.

As Ruth and Abdul approached her friends, she had an urge to scream out, "Call the police! He raped me!" but stifled it by tensing in her throat; she feared the reaction of the crowd.

As Ruth had a Middle Eastern girlfriend in her current life, I suggested that she ask her about the cultural attitudes involved here. Ruth received a lot of insight from her friend and realized that a Middle Eastern crowd would have considered Ruth, a young European woman accusing a local man of rape, to be a whore. At best they would have ignored her; at worst they would have accused her or beat her. The police, the friend was sure, would not have taken the situation seriously. They might even have arrested Ruth, instead. This cultural insight was critical in alleviating Ruth's guilt for not having sought help or retribution.

Upon returning to her memories, I had Ruth sense what she had to do in her body to make herself hold the rapist's hand and not cry out: it was a difficult feat. She had to tense her arm while relaxing her hand, tense her throat, not run, etc. At the same time I encouraged her to consider how smart she had been—how she had likely saved herself additional harm, shame, and anguish by controlling herself in these ways.

Now Ruth became angry at the rapist and how he had set her up. Previously, she had always been angry only at herself. She was ready to separate her responsibility from his, realizing that it was he who was in the wrong. (She knew—and we still needed to work on—that there was something amiss in her judgment that she walked into the situation. But she realized at this point that the responsibility for the rape itself clearly was Abdul's.) Ruth had clearly said "No!" to his sexual advances. Then, for the first time since the incident, Ruth remembered that Abdul had attempted to strangle her when she resisted.

This was an important step. It was crucial to assign guilt. Many trauma survivors are all too ready to take all blame, and many therapists are too quick to place all blame on the offender. For the client to reclaim his or her power and sanity, the truth of guilt must be illuminated. A rapist is responsible for a rape. Period. And the victim of rape must be willing to look at how he or she came into the situation—not to feel guilty, but so that he or she can prevent the same from happening in the future.

Ruth expressed her anger and cried that it was not fair that Abdul got off free and she had suffered all these years. I suggested that she allow herself a fantasy of what she would have liked to have happen. She was very quick and clear: he should have been caught, tried, and castrated. "Men who can't contain their sexual hormones shouldn't be allowed to have them." She was sure she didn't want him killed and didn't want him to suffer pain, just be deprived of the hormones that she saw as the cause of what he did to her.

Ruth now felt different. For the first time since the rape she didn't feel ashamed for having been raped. Instead she felt angry at the rapist.

This was the pivotal turn in Ruth's therapy. The rest was much easier. When she worked with the rape itself, Ruth was not plagued with shame and doubts about who was in the wrong. And when she approached looking at how she got herself into that situation, the shame of the rape itself was separated from her guilt for not having been more cautious.

BRIDGING THE IMPLICIT AND THE EXPLICIT

When PTSD splits mind and body, implicitly remembered images, emotions, somatic sensations, and behaviors become disengaged from explicitly stored

facts and meanings about the traumatic event(s)—whether they are consciously remembered or not. Healing trauma requires a linking of all aspects
of a traumatic event. The implicit and the explicit must be bridged in order to
create a cohesive narration of those events, as well as to place them in their
proper slot in the client's past. Making sense of implicitly encoded sensations,
emotions, and behaviors in the context of the traumatic memory is a crucial
part of this process. The tools for creating this bridge are to be found in both
psychotherapy and body-psychotherapy. It is necessary to address what occurs
in the body, and it is equally necessary to use words to make sense of and
describe the experience. The bottom line is that clients need to be helped to
think and feel concurrently—that is, to be able to sense their sensations, emotions, and behaviors while formulating coherent conclusions about the relationship between those and the images and thoughts that accompany them.
Finally, a cohesive narrative of the traumatic incident will take form and the
event will come to occupy its proper place in the client's past.

The two therapy sessions presented below illustrate the integration that is
possible with trauma therapy when both dimensions—mind and body—are
included. As before, therapists are encouraged to think about which elements
might enhance their own ways of working.

Gail, Part II

Gail's first therapy session to resolve an earlier car accident was described at
the end of Chapter 6. What follows is the transcript of a subsequent session.

> T: What do you want to work on today?
> G: Someone recently asked me how I got the scars on my arm and
> it made me feel light headed and nauseous. I got a very clear
> image of the end of the accident, when the car stopped rolling
> and I looked down and saw that my left arm was broken.
> T: What are you feeling in your body as you talk about that now?
> G: Slightly anxious here (she points toward her belly) and a funny
> feeling in my jaw, a slight shaking.
> T: How's our distance?
> *(I remembered her tendency to dissociate.)*

G: (She smiles.) It's fine.

T: Tell me what you remember about your anchor.

(It is important to recheck the anchor at each session. Sometimes it will need to be changed or altered.)

G: It's at a place near my friend's house in a beautifully forested valley with a crystal-clear shallow river; you can see the rocks in the bottom. There's a particular granite rock I like to sit on.

T: What are you feeling in your body right now?

G: My stomach is looser and my shoulders have dropped, my hands are dry.

(Parasympathetic signs mean the nervous system is relaxed; it is safe to proceed.)

T: Then let's get to it. Okay?

G: Okay.

T: Where do you want to start?

(Giving the client control.)

G: I want to tell you what happened when the car stopped moving. It was then I first realized I was still here, still alive. I looked down and saw that my forearm was bent [broken], and I straightened it. It was as if I could not bear it being bent like that.

T: What are you feeling as you talk about this?

G: Nothing, no feeling, but somewhere in me I know it was really scary.

T: What is that like to know it was scary but not feel it?

(Gail has dissociated her fear. I want to know how she regards the incongruence. A client should not be pushed to feel dissociated feelings.)

G: It's weird. I don't like it. I want to put those two things together.

T: Which two things?

G: Feeling scared about my arm.

T: Don't assume that it needs to be BIG scary.

(Gail is afraid to feel her fear and I do not want her to imagine it any bigger than it is. Sometimes emotions are dissociated because of the fear they will be overwhelming. Trauma clients usually expect dramatic expressions of emotion. The fact is that sometimes they are very subtle.)

T: What do you feel in your body right now?

G: I feel my shoulder more.

T: It looks like you are moving. Are you?

G: I'm twisting to the right.

T: Do you want to follow that? See if you can stay behind the impulse. Just follow it. (She twists more to her right.) What happens when you do that?

G: I remember wanting to throw my arms around my boyfriend and feel him there, but he was unconscious. (She begins to speak faster, and her voice tone rises.) Then this policeman came to my window and I yelled, "Get me out of here!" I was afraid the car would explode. And . . .

T: Wait. Slow down. Tell me what you are feeling right now.

(She's starting to be swept away by her narrative. We have to apply the brakes, to prevent overwhelm or retraumatization.)

G: I feel kind of shaky, teary.

T: Do you know what the emotion is?

(At this point I do not want her to sink into the emotion. She's too dubious for that. I want her to know what it is before she feels it strongly, so it will be more familiar, and hopefully more digestible.)

G: Frightened. And a bit like, I can't think of the word, like something has to be taken care of right now—urgent.

T: How does that feel in your body?

G: Shaky. And I have an impulse to get up, to move.

(Many feelings and sensations are being remembered at once.)

T: Follow the impulse.

G: I don't feel like I can. What I want to do is tell you how the policeman wouldn't let me do that. He wasn't letting me get up and out. He was doing all the right things. He said, "Hang on. Can you feel your feet? Can you feel your legs? Do you have any pain in your back?" But I kept saying, "I just want to get out of here. I'm okay. Get me out of here!" But he was making me go through all these things.

T: Do you know why he was doing that?

(Reality checking.)

G: He wanted to make sure I didn't have a back injury. But I knew

I didn't. I'd already checked that, myself. I'd done that bit!! I'd already done that and I just wanted to get out of there.

T: What are you feeling now?

G: Angry. I want to say, "Shut up! I know it is safe to move me, get me out of here."

T: Do you remember and/or know how long it was from the time he got to you till he helped you out of the car.

(Another reality check. At the time it probably felt like an eternity.)

G: I don't think it was very long.

T: What are you feeling in your body now?

G: A bit calmer. I feel a slight trembling in my legs.

(Trembling often accompanies a release of fear, but it is not time to focus on it yet as she is not very connected with it.)

T: What is happening with your hands and arms?

G: (She looks down.) My right hand is holding my left arm. That's what I did then: I braced my broken arm.

(Visual cues and kinesthetic nerves help the body to remember a posture central to Gail's memory of the trauma.)

T: How does that feel?

G: I can feel something in my throat, but I don't know what it is.

T: How's the distance between you and me?

G: It's fine.

T: Does it feel okay to go on? I'm aware I'm not taking you to the anchor, but it seems this level of arousal is tolerable for you.

(Checking to see if she is dissociating. A lot is going on and she does not seem very hyperaroused. It is usually the case that when emotions are integrated, hyperarousal is reduced, but it's a good idea to check.)

G: Yes, that's fine.

T: What are you aware of in your arms?

G: I don't want to take my right arm away from my left [broken] arm.

T: You don't seem to look at your left arm. Is that right?

G: Yes. I don't want to, but there's something there.

T: You don't have to.

G: It's okay, I will.

T: Don't do it yet. When you do, I suggest you just take a little peek at a time. Take just one peek and see what happens.

(*Taking a small, controlled bite.*)

G: (She glances quickly.)

T: What happened?

G: I felt a shiver go through my body.

T: All the way through?

G: Yeah. It feels like: oohhhh, it was horrible. (The shivering increases.)

T: Let that trembling happen.

(*There is more connection to the fear now, and more chance for integration.*)

G: I feel kind of sick.

T: See if it's okay to stay with the trembling and sick feeling a minute or so. (She does and the trembling subsides.)

T: How are you feeling?

G: Calmer, but still a bit sick.

T: Don't you think that's a normal reaction? When someone sees a broken limb in an unnatural position, you get a bit of a sick feeling.

G: Oh, yeah! It looked awful. Uuuh. (More shaking.)

T: How does the shaking feel?

G: It feels quite good actually.

(*She is integrating this memory: images, sensations, and feelings.*)

T: Don't make it more or less, just let it do its thing. What happens to the sick feeling when you shake like that? Does it get more or less?

G: It gets less.

T: How's our distance?

G: Okay

T: The same?

G: Only a slight pulling back.

(*Slight dissociation. Time to put on the brakes and use the anchor.*)

T: Let's take a little break.

G: (Laughs with relief.)

T: What kind of trees are in your place?

G: Oak.

T: Is oak the kind of tree that has those little helicopters that fall spinning?

G: No, that's maple. Oaks have acorns!

T: Oh, yeah, that's right. (We both laugh.)

(*Laughter is a great remedy for hyperaousal and dissociation.*)

T: Are you usually there when leaves are on the trees, or not?

G: I've been there with both.

T: All seasons? Have you seen the leaves turn colors, too?

G: Yes.

T: What are you aware of in your body?

G: Relief. Less tension.

T: Do you ever go barefoot in the stream?

(*Associating various sensations connected to the anchor.*)

G: Oh, yeah! All the time. Well, not all the time. Even in the winter just to get my toes wet.

T: How does that feel?

G: It's incredibly cleansing. And very cold. But it really can clean out anything. (She sighs deeply.)

T: Can you feel yourself breathing?

G: Yes.

T: Do you want to stay there for a while, or is it time to go back?

G: Stay a little while. I feel a rock under me.

(*The client takes control.*)

T: What else?

G: I can hear the sound of the water running around me.

T: Have you ever shown your rock to a friend?

G: Not this one. Other ones, yes. But this one is too special to me. Now I'm ready to go back.

(*The more the client is in control, the more courage she gathers to face the frightening past.*)

T: When you think of your arm, what do you feel in your body?

G: I feel myself tilt to the right and pull back from seeing it.

T: Can you describe that further?

G: Yeah. It's weird. It feels like if I leaned to the left, I'd get very emotional.

T: And when you lean to the right?

G: There I feel nothing, like when I thought, "I'm not going to let anyone see me like that," and I straightened my arm. And I was "okay" from then on.

T: And when you moved your arm in that state, what did it feel like?

G: Nothing. No pain. No feeling. Entirely numb.

T: So you partially dissociated to accomplish an important task.
(Recognizing the resource in the defense.)

G: Yes. I was afraid the bone would rip through my skin if it was left like that when I was moved. But the doctors didn't like that I had done it.

T: You were doing everything you could do to protect yourself. To accomplish that you had to make some kind of internal split, which looks to be off to your right.

G: Yes, and back. It's definitely back.

T: To your right and back. Can you feel yourself in that place now?

G: Sort of, but I haven't moved completely into it. I'm hovering in the middle.

T: I'm quite aware of your hands. Are you aware of anything with your hands?

G: They're shaking.

T: *They?*

G: Well, actually my left one is shaking and my right one is not.

T: Exactly.

G: It's like the left one is holding the fear.

T: And the right?

G: It's like the right one is more steady, "I can handle this."
(The right and left hands are representing the right and left split that is occurring between feeling and numbing.)

T: I'm going to suggest that you put your awareness in both hands at the same time. Can you do that?

G: Yes.

T: Good. Keep your awareness in both while moving them closer together, *very* slowly.

(The movement symbolizes integration of the feeling and the numb parts of her.)

G: (Trembles as she does this.)

T: Do you feel your shaking?

G: Yes. (She slowly continues.)

T: What's happening?

G: I feel angry. There's something about me taking care of myself and others not taking care of me. Like that I straightened my arm and made myself okay.

T: What's happening in your eyes?

G: I'm getting tearful, sad.

T: Do you know why?

(Can she make sense of her sensations and feelings—think while she is feeling?)

G: It wasn't that they didn't take care of me. I wouldn't *let* them take care of me. I kept telling everybody I was okay.

T: What was the truth?

G: Of what I did or how I felt?

T: Of how you felt.

G: I felt really scared. (She starts to cry and her voice gets softer and rises an octave.) The car went out of control and rolled over and over . . .

(She's integrating the image of the accident with the dissociated emotion.)

T: . . . and you were really scared . . .

G: . . . and I was really scared. It was like it turned over in slow motion so it seemed like it took hours, and I didn't know where it was going to land.

T: . . . and you were really scared . . .

(Encouraging her to stay connected to the fear while she is remembering. A big step in healing of trauma takes place when the client feels safe enough, now, to feel the previously dissociated fear.)

G: . . . and I was really scared. I was *really* scared!

T: Do you feel that right now?

G: Yeah. (She trembles.)

T: I can see it. Just let the trembling happen.

(*With more connection to the fear, the trembling will be more effective in releasing it.*)

G: And . . .

T: Slow down. See if it is okay to stay with the feeling in your body a bit longer. (G trembles a bit more.)

G: I can feel I'm beginning to get angry now. I want to tell you about it. What was most unhelpful is what the policeman said. He came over and the first thing out of his mouth was (G's voice becomes stronger), "Wow, when I arrived and saw this car, I thought I was just going to be picking up pieces!" And (she gets even louder with tears in her voice) I DIDN'T NEED TO HEAR THAT!

T: That scared you more.

G: Yes! I really, really didn't need to hear that!

T: See if you can stay connected to the anger and at the same time feel how much his words scared you.

G: No. I'm not going to feel how much that scared me.

T: Okay. What are you feeling in your body right now?

G: Solid on my seat. A little gone away though.

T: Do you know why?

G: I think because I don't want to feel that fear.

T: Did you ever tell anyone how scared you were?

G: No, I was "okay." I told everyone how lucky I was that I survived. I never told anyone I was scared.

T: Could you tell anyone, now?

G: That might be hard. Maybe my best friend.

T: Can you imagine telling her?

G: I know I *could* tell her, but I don't know if I could *feel* anything.

T: Would you like to try?

G: Yes.

T: Do you know why I am suggesting this?

(*It is not a guessing game. I want to know if she is thinking and able to follow my motivation. I will tell her if she does not know.*)

G: Because I haven't had any contact or support about it.

T: Exactly. It seems you've been much alone with that fear.

G: Yes, I have.

T: Okay, are you game?

G: Yes, I'd like to.

T: So, in your mind, imagine being together with your friend. Where would you two be?

G: In my kitchen. Just imagining it, I can feel I'm shaking a little.

T: Just let that happen. (She does and also cries for a while. Then the tears and shaking subside.) What do you want to tell your friend?

G: (With a lot of emotion) I was *so* scared. I thought I was going to die. Then this stupid policeman comes and tells me he thought I was dead! I got so angry. What a stupid thing to say!

T: You didn't die, but you were very scared.

G: That seems like a good thing to mention! (Laughs) And I didn't! I didn't die. I actually wasn't even that hurt.

T: But, you were scared you were going to die.

G: Physically, I wasn't very hurt. But, boy, I was scared I was going to die!

T: What are you feeling in your body?

G: Really awake. More calm. And my heart's stopped racing.

T: Do you think you could really tell your friend?

G: Yes. Actually, I want to. I think I'll call her when I get home.

(*Making a bridge between therapy and the client's daily life is very important. If the therapy is not relevant to current functioning then it is not worth much.*)

T: How are you feeling in your body now?

G: Quite calm, actually.

T: If it's okay, I'd like you to try looking at your left arm again.

(G looks at her arm.) What happens?

(*Checking to see how much has been integrated and relieved.*)

G: I feel a bit sad seeing those scars, but I'm not feeling sick or scared.

T: Do you know what the sadness is about?

G: I'm just sorry my arm was hurt and I didn't tell anyone I was scared.

T: I can well understand that. Does this feel like a good place to stop?

G: Yes it does.

Commencing with a traumatic trigger, the scars on her arm, Gail was able to recognize and integrate the most frightening events of the car accident. Gradually, she made sense of somatic sensations, emotions, and movements in the context of the visual and auditory memory images that occurred. One of the most important insights was the acknowledgment of how alone she was and has been with the frightening memories of that accident. Talking with her best friend about it will initiate a new behavior in Gail's current life. Hopefully, the next time she is scared she'll be able to tell someone. By the end of the session, Gail was able to return to the original stimulus—looking at her arm—with absolutely no hyperarousal.

CHARLIE AND THE DOG, THE FINAL EPISODE

This case was introduced in Chapter 1 and was used to weave a thread through the Theory section. In Chapter 6 it was used to illustrate how simple body awareness could calm a seriously hyperaroused state. Charlie and the Dog will now be concluded as an example of the importance of linking the implicit to the explicit. Here both reality checking and attention to somatic impulses assist in changing the reaction to a traumatic trigger.

When Charlie could sense his body (and this had helped him to calm substantially—all signs of sympathetic activation were decreasing except his dry mouth), he was ready to think. I asked him, "Is Ruff anything like the dog that attacked you?" Startled, he answered, "I don't know, I never looked at Ruff." This was amazing to everyone in the group, as Charlie had been around Ruff several times over the preceding two years. However, Charlie had managed to avoid Ruff completely. He became quite anxious just at the thought of looking at Ruff. I encouraged him by suggesting that he take just a very quick peek through his fingers (as a shy child might do). He did it very fast—with the speed of a camera shutter—just long enough to snap a visual image of Ruff. At that point Charlie exclaimed with great surprise, "My goodness! Ruff doesn't look anything like that dog who attacked me!" With that realization he calmed down considerably, the stiffness melting from his body and sympathetic excitation further decreased. It was a very dramatic response. Both he and I waited and watched the melting happen, checking body awareness from time to time. When the stiffness had fully melted, his legs gradually became restless—it was easy to see the little tick-like movements that developed in his thighs and shins. I brought his attention to the movements, what Levine (1992) would call intentional movements (slight muscle contractions that may indicate a behavioral intention that has not been fulfilled) and I encouraged him to sense them from the inside (through the interoceptive, kinesthetic nerves). I suspected the movements would develop further if we were patient, and they did. After a couple more minutes Charlie felt the impulse to curl his legs away from where Ruff had been sitting. He did that, and remarked, rather pleased, "I can move like this if Ruff comes back. Then she couldn't put her head on my knee." Charlie then found he had a further impulse to get up and walk a couple of meters away, which he did saying, "I could also walk away if Ruff comes back." (As obvious as that might seem, in Charlie's hyperaroused state, there had been no such option.) At this point I checked Charlie's body awareness again; all signs of hyperarousal were gone.

Later in the workshop Charlie had the opportunity to exercise his new tools as Ruff did, indeed, come again to sit by him—twice. The first time Charlie was able to turn away from Ruff without being triggered into flashback, though he reported that he was a bit anxious. By the second time, Charlie just curled his legs away from Ruff, who settled herself nearby. This time Charlie felt no anxiety whatsoever. We never addressed the details of Charlie's trauma of being attacked by a dog. Instead we facilitated body awareness, reality testing, and the development of new behavioral resources. I met Charlie some time after that workshop and he reported to me that he no longer froze or broke into a cold sweat when seeing dogs behind windows or even meeting them on the street, though he maintained a high level of caution with the type of dog that had attacked him. A few years later I saw Charlie again and he proudly told me that he and his family had adopted a dog and welcomed it into their home. It was the frosting on his sweet victory.

The implicit memories represented by Charlie's stiff tonic immobility, dry mouth, accelerated heart rate, and the sensation of Ruff's head on his thigh were integrated with his factual, explicit memory ("*I was attacked by a dog*"). Explicit processes were engaged to identify here-and-now reality as separate from the past ("*Ruff doesn't look anything like the dog who attacked me*"). New behaviors (curling the legs to one side, getting up and walking away) were also encoded in both implicit memory (through practice) and explicit memory (through describing and making sense of both old and new behaviors).

The body remembers traumatic events through the encoding in the brain of sensations, movements, and emotions that are associated with trauma. Healing PTS and PTSD necessitates attention to what is happening in the body as well as the interpretations being made in the mind. Language bridges the mind/body gap, linking explicit and implicit memories. Somatic memory becomes personal history when the impact of traumatic events are so weakened that the events can finally be placed in their proper point in the client's past.

THE FAR SIDE   by Gary Larson

THE FAR SIDE © 1990 FARWORKS, INC. Used by permission. All rights reserved.

References

American Psychiatric Association. (1980). *Diagnostic and statistical manual of mental disorders* (3rd ed.). Washington DC: Author.

American Psychiatric Association. (1994). *Diagnostic and statistical manual of mental disorders* (4th ed.). Washington DC: Author.

Andrews, B. (1997). Forms of memory recovery among adults in therapy: Preliminary results from an in-depth survey. In J. D. Read & D. S. Lindsay (Eds.), *Recollections of trauma: Scientific evidence and clinical practice* (pp. 455–460). New York: Plenum.

Azar, B. (1998). Why can't this man feel whether or not he's standing up? *APA Monitor, 29*(6), 18–20.

Bandler, R., & Grinder, J. (1979). *Frogs into princes*. Moab, UT: Real People.

Bauer, M., Priebe, S., & Graf, K. J. (1994). Psychological and endocrine abnormalities in refugees from East Germany, part II: Serum levels of cortisol, prolactin, luteinizing hormone, follicle stimulating hormone and testosterone. *Psychiatry Research, 51*, 75–85.

Begley, S. (1999, Spring/Summer). Understanding perimenopause. *Newsweek, Special Issue*, 30–33.

Bloch, G. (1985). *Body and self: Elements of human biology, behavior and health*. Los Altos: William Kaufmann.

Bodynamic Institute Training Program, 1988–1992, Copenhagen, Denmark: Author.

Bremner, J. D., Randall, P. K., Scott, T. M., Bronen, R. A., Seibyl, J. P., Southwick, S. M., Delaney, R. C., McCarthy, G., Charney, D. S., & Innis, R. B. (1997). Magnetic resonance imaging-based measurement of hippocampal volume in posttraumatic stress disorder related to childhood physical and sexual abuse: a preliminary report. *Biological Psychiatry, 41*(1), 23–32.

Bremner, J. D., Southwick, S., Brett, E., Fontana, A., Rosenheck, R., & Charney, D. S. (1992). Dissociation and posttraumatic stress disorder in vietnam combat veterans. *American Journal of Psychiatry, 149*, 328–332.

Breslau, N., Davis, G. C., Andreski, P., & Peterson, E. (1991). Traumatic events and posttraumatic stress disorder in an urban population of young adults. *Archives of General Psychiatry, 48*(3), 216–222.

Brett, E. A. (1996). The classification of posttraumatic stress disorder. In B. A. van der Kolk, A. C. McFarlane, & L. Weisaeth (Eds.), *Traumatic stress* (pp. 117–128). New York: Guilford.

Claparede, E. (1951). Recognition and "me-ness." In D. Rapaport (Ed.), *Organization and pathology of thought* (pp. 58–75). New York: Columbia University Press. (Original work published 1911)

Classen, C., Koopman, C., & Spiegel, D. (1993). Trauma and dissociation. *Bulletin of the Menninger Clinic, 57*(2), 178–194.

Damasio, A. R. (1994). *Descartes' error.* New York: Putnam.

Darwin, C. (1872/1965). *The expression of the emotions in man and animals.* Chicago: University of Chicago Press. (Original work published 1872)

De Bellis, M. D., Keshavan, M. S., Clark, D. B., Casey, B. J., Giedd, J. N., Boring, A. M., Frustaci, K., & Ryan, N. D. (1999). Developmental traumatology, part II: Brain development. *Biological Psychiatry, 45*(10), 1271–1284.

Duggal, S., & Sroufe, L. A. (1998). Recovered memory of childhood sexual trauma: A documented case from a longitudinal study. *Journal of Traumatic Stress, 11*(2), 301–321.

Eich, J. E. (1980). The cue-dependent nature of state-dependent retrieval. *Memory and Cognition, 8*(2), 157–173.

Elliott, D. M. (1997). Traumatic events: Prevalence and delayed recall in the general population. *Journal of Consulting and Clinical Psychology, 65*(8), 811–820.

Ferenczi, S. (1949). Confusion of tongues between the adult and the child. *International Journal of Psychoanalysis, 30,* 225–230. (Paper originally read at the 12th International Psychoanalytical Congress, Wiesbaden, September 1932)

Gallup, G. G., & Maser, J. D. (1977). Tonic immobility: Evolutionary underpinnings of human catalepsy and catatonia. In M. E. P. Seligman & J. D. Maser (Eds.), *Psychopathology: Experimental models* (pp. 334–357). San Francisco: W. H. Freeman.

Grafton, S. (1990). *"G" is for gumshoe.* New York: Ballantine.

Goulding, M. M., & Goulding, R. L. (1997). *Changing lives through redecision therapy* (Rev. ed.). New York: Grove.

Gunnar, M. R., & Barr, Ronald G. (1998). Stress, early brain development, and behavior. *Infants and Young Children, 11*(1), 1–14.

Heide, F. J., & Borkovec, T. D. (1984). Relaxation-induced anxiety: Mechanisms and theoretical implications. *Behavioral Research and Therapy, 22*(1), 1–12.

Heide, F. J., & Borkovec, T. D. (1983). Relaxation-induced anxiety: Paradoxical anxiety enhancement due to relaxation training. *Journal of Consulting and Clinical Psychology, 51*(2), 171–182.

Herman, J. L. (1992). *Trauma and recovery.* New York: Basic.

Hovdestad, W. E., & Kristiansen, C. M. (1996). Mind meets body: On the nature of recovered memories of trauma. *Women and Therapy, 19*(1), 31–45.

International Society for Traumatic Stress Studies. (1998). *Childhood trauma remembered: A report on the current scientific knowledge base and its applications*. Northbrook, IL: Author.

Jacobsen, R., & Edinger, J. D. (1982). Side effects of relaxation treatment. *American Journal of Psychiatry, 13*(7), 952–953.

Janet, P. (1887). L'Anesthésie systematisée et la dissociation des phénomemés psychologiques [Systematized anesthesia and the psychological phenomenon of dissociation]. *Revue Philosophique, 23*(1), 449–472.

Jørgensen, S. (1992). Bodynamic analytic work with shock/post-traumatic stress. *Energy and Character, 23*(2), 30–46.

Kulka, R. A., Schlenger, W. E., Fairbank, J. A., Hough, R. L., Jordan, B. K., Marmar, C. R., & Weiss, D. S., (1990). *Trauma and the Vietnam war generation: Report of findings from the National Vietnam Veterans Readjustment Study*. New York: Brunner/Mazel.

LeDoux, J. E. (1996). *The emotional brain*. New York: Simon & Schuster.

Lehrer, P. M., & Woolfolk, R. L. (1993). Specific effects of stress management techniques. In P. M. Lehrer & R. L. Woolfolk (Eds.), *Principles and practice of stress management* (pp. 481–520). New York: Guilford.

Levine, P. (1992). *The body as healer: Transforming trauma and anxiety*. Lyons, CO: Author.

Levine, P. (1997). *Waking the tiger*. Berkeley, CA: North Atlantic.

Lindy, J. D., Green, B. L., & Grace, M. (1992). Somatic reenactment in the treatment of posttraumatic stress disorder. *Psychotherapy and Psychosomatics, 57*, 180–186.

Loewenstein, R. J. (1993). Dissociation, development and the psychobiology of trauma, *Journal of the American Academy of Psychoanalysis, 21*(4), 581–603.

Malt, U. F., & Weisaeth, L. (1989). Disaster psychiatry and traumatic stress studies in Norway. *Acta Psychiatrica Scandinavia, 355*(Suppl.), 7–12.

Marmar, C. R., Weiss, D. S., Metzler, T. J., & Delucchi, K. (1996). Characteristics of emergency services personnel related to peritraumatic dissociations during critical incident exposure. *American Journal of Psychiatry, 153*(Festschrift suppl.), 94–102.

Nadel, L. (1994). Multiple memory systems: What and why, an update. In D. L. Schacter & E. Tulving (Eds.), *Memory systems* (pp. 39–63). Cambridge: MIT Press.

Nadel, L., & Jacobs, W. J. (1996). The role of the hippocampus in PTSD, panic, and phobia. In N. Kato (Ed.), *Hippocampus: Functions and clinical relevance* (pp. 455–463). Amsterdam: Elsevier.

Nadel, L., & Zola-Morgan, S. (1984). Infantile amnesia. In M. Moscovitch (Ed.), *Infantile memory* (pp. 145–172). New York: Plenum.

Napier, N. (1996). *Recreating your self: Increasing self-esteem through imaging and self-hypnosis*. New York: Norton.

Nathanson, D. L. (1992). *Shame and pride: Affect, sex, and the birth of the self*. New York: Norton.

Pavlov, I. P. (1960). *Conditioned reflexes.* New York: Dover. (Original work published 1927)

Penfield, W., & Perot, P. (1963). The brain's record of auditory and visual experience. *Brain, 86,* 595–696.

Perls, F. (1942). *Ego, hunger and aggression.* Durban, South Africa: Knox.

Perls, F. (1969). *In and out of the garbage pail.* Moab, UT: Real People.

Perry, B. D., Pollard, R. A., Blakley, T. L., Baker, W. L., & Vigilante, D. (1995). Childhood trauma, the neurobiology of adaptation, and "use-dependent" development of the brain: How "states" become "traits." *Infant Mental Health Journal, 16*(4), 271–291.

Rauch, S. L., Shin, L. M., Wahlen, P. J. H., & Pitman, R. K. (1998). Neuroimaging and the neuroanatomy of posttraumatic stress disorder. *CNS Spectrums, 3*(7) (Supple. 2), 31–41.

Reus, V. I., Weingartner, H., & Post, R. M. (1979). Clinical implications of state-dependent learning. *American Journal of Psychiatry, 136*(7), 927–931.

Rothschild, B. (1993). A shock primer for the bodypsychotherapist. *Energy and Character, 24*(1), 33–38.

Rothschild, B. (1995a). Defining shock and trauma in body-psychotherapy. *Energy and Character, 26*(2), 61–65.

Rothschild, B. (1995b). *Defense, resource and choice.* Presentation at The 5th European Congress of Body-Psychotherapy, Carry-Le Rouet, France.

Rothschild, B. (1996/97). An annotated trauma case history: Somatic trauma therapy, part I. *Somatics, 11*(1), 48–53.

Rothschild, B. (1997). An annotated trauma case history: Somatic trauma therapy, part II. *Somatics, 11*(2), 44–49.

Rothschild, B. (1999). Making trauma therapy safe. *Self and Society, 27*(2), 17–23.

Sapolsky, R. (1994). *Why zebras don't get ulcers.* New York: W. H. Freeman.

Schacter, D. (1996). *Searching for memory.* New York: Basic.

Schore, A. (1994). *Affect regulation and the origin of the self.* Hillsdale, NJ: Lawrence Erlbaum.

Schore, A. (1996). The experience-dependent maturation of a regulatory system in the orbital prefrontal cortex and the origin of developmental psychopathology. *Development and Psychopathology, 8,* 59–87.

Schuff, N., Marmar, C. R., Weiss, D. S., Neylan, T., Schoenfeld, F. B., Fein, G., & Weiner, M. W. (1997). Reduced hippocampal volume and n-acetyl aspartate in posttraumatic stress disorder. *Annals of the New York Academy of Sciences, 821,* 516–520.

Scott, M. J., & Stradling, S. G. (1994). Post-traumatic stress disorder without the trauma. *British Journal of Clinical Psychology, 33*(1), 71–74.

Selye, H. (1984). *The stress of life.* New York: McGraw-Hill.

Siegel, D. J. (1996). Cognition, memory and dissociation. *Child and Adolescent Psychiatric Clinics of North America, 5*(2), 509–536.

Siegel, D. J. (1999). *The developing mind*. New York: Guilford.

Skinner, B. F. (1961). Teaching machines. *Scientific American, 205*(5), 90–107.

Squire, L. R. (1987). *Memory and brain*, New York: Oxford University Press.

Stevens, J. O. (1971). *Awareness: Exploring, experimenting, experiencing*. Moab, UT: Real People.

Suarez, S. D., & Gallup, G. G. (1979). Tonic immobility as a response to rape in humans: A theoretical note. *Psychological Record, 29*, 315–320.

Tavris, C. (1998, June 21). A widening gulf splits lab and couch. *The New York Times*.

Terr, L. (1994). *Unchained memories*. New York: Basic.

van der Hart, O., & Friedman, B. (1989). A reader's guide to Pierre Janet on dissociation: A neglected intellectual heritage. *Dissociation, 2*(1), 3–16.

van der Hart, O., & Nijenhuis, E. R. S. (1999). Bearing witness to uncorroborated trauma: The clinician's development of reflective belief. *Professional Psychology: Research and Practice, 30*(1), 37–44.

van der Hart, O. & Steele, K. (1997). Relieving or reliving childhood trauma? A commentary on Miltenburg and Singer. *Theory and Psychology, 9*(4), 533–540.

van der Kolk, B. A. (1987). *Psychological trauma*. Washington, DC: American Psychiatric.

van der Kolk, B. A. (1994). The body keeps the score. *Harvard Review of Psychiatry, 1*, 253–265.

van der Kolk, B. A. (1998, November). *Neurobiology, attachment and trauma*. Presentation at the annual meeting of the International Society for Traumatic Stress Studies, Washington, D.C.

van der Kolk, B. A., Brown, P., & van der Hart, O. (1989). Pierre Janet on post-traumatic stress. *Journal of Traumatic Stress, 2*(4), 365–377.

van der Kolk, B. A., McFarlane, A. C., & Weisaeth, L. (1996). (Eds.). *Traumatic stress*. New York: Guilford.

Wahlberg, L., van der Kolk, B. A., Brett, E., & Marmar, C. R. (1996, November). *PTSD: Anxiety disorder or dissociative disorder?* Symposium conducted at the annual meeting of the International Society for Traumatic Stress Studies, San Francisco.

Williams, L. M. (1995). Recovered memories of abuse in women with documented child sexual victimization histories. *Journal of Traumatic Stress, 8*(4), 649–673.

Wolpe, J. (1969). *The practice of behavior therapy*. New York: Pergamon.

Yehuda, R., Southwick, S. M., Nussbaum, G., Wahby, V., Giller, E. L. Jr., & Mason, J. W. (1990). Low urinary cortisol excretion in patients with posttraumatic stress disorder. *Journal of Nervous and Mental Disease, 178*, 366–369.

Yehuda R., Kahana, B., Binder-Brynes, K., Southwick, S., Zemelman, S., Mason, J. W., & Giller, E. L., (1995). Low urinary cortisol excretion in Holocaust survivors with posttraumatic stress disorder. *American Journal of Psychiatry, 152*, 982–986.

Yehuda, R., Teicher, M. H., Levengood, R., Trestman, R., & Siever, L. J. (1996). Cortisol regulation in posttraumatic stress disorder and major depression: A chronobiological analysis. *Biological Psychiatry, 40,* 79–88.

Index

as an anchor, 95
reinforcing with body awareness, 107
safety
foundations of, in trauma therapy, 98–99
removing triggers, Rodney (case), 87–88
in the therapeutic relationship, 83
in therapy, 87–88
Sapolsky, R., 18
scale, of arousal to hyperarousal, 111–12
Schacter, D., 27, 28
Schoenfeld, F. B., 22
Schore, S., xiii, 17, 22, 23, 24, 80, 82, 84
Schuff, N., 22
Scott, M. J., 81
self-forgiveness, 12
Selye, H., 7
sensations, safe, distinguishing, 106
sensory nervous system, 37–45
cues from, and body awareness, 101–2
exteroceptive, 39–40, 45
sensory cues, 73
interoceptive, 39–40
kinesthetic sense, 164
sensory cues, 73
vestibular sense, 43–44
see also proprioceptive system
sensory stimulus, in utero, 23
session closure, mitigating, 148–49
sexual dysfunction, in posttraumatic stress
disorder, 7
shame
as disappointment in the self, 62–63
from freezing in response to threat, 11
positive side of, 62–63
in rape, 159
in sexual abuse, 62
from tonic immobility, 50
and visual boundaries, 146
Shame and Pride (Nathanson), 154
shaping behavior, with operant conditioning, 34
Shin, L. M., 22
SIBAM dissociation model, 67–70, 118
Siegel, D. J., xiii, 17, 24
Siever, L. J., 9
skin level boundaries, 143–45
establishing, 146
Skinner, B. F., 33–34
skin tone, observing in therapy, 109
sleep disturbances, in posttraumatic stress
disorder, 7

socialization
in the relationship between caretaker and
child, 24
and the survival value of shame, 63
somatic disturbance, in posttraumatic stress
disorder, 7
somatic interventions, for trauma therapy, 5,
129–49
somatic markers, 107
new, in successful therapy, 82
theory of, 43, 59–60
somatic memory, 19
body awareness as a step toward interpreting, 101
Donna (case), 117–18
as personal history, 150–73
reliability of, xv
as a resource, 118–19
Tom (case), 119
sensations for making sense of, 117–18
and the senses, 44
understanding, 37–64
somatic nervous system (SomNS), 37–38,
50–56
movements caused by, using to facilitate
recall, 55
somatic symptoms, 82
Southwick, S. M., 9, 13
Spiegel, D., 13
spiritual resources, 91
split awareness, forms of, 13, see also dissociation
Squire, L. R., 27
Sroufe, L. A., 152
state-dependent recall, 35–36, 44, 55–56, 73
Steele, K., 78
Stevens, J. O., 101
stimulus, exteroceptive, example, 46
storage, of memory, 27
Stradling, S. G., 81
stress
defined, 7
medications that mimic body response in,
154
traumatic, defined, 7
stress inoculation, 35
Suarez, S. D., 50
Subjective Units of Disturbance Scale (SUDS),
110
survival/survival responses, 46–47
of affects, 62–63